SAUSALITO
Cooking with a View

FAVORITE RECIPES FROM THE
SAUSALITO WOMAN'S CLUB

Since 1913 the Sausalito Woman's Club has been a major civic and cultural force in Sausalito. Its membership of 300 is firmly committed to public service through charitable donations and hands-on participation in civic enhancement, emergency awareness, youth programs, historic preservation, conservation and the environment. Over 40 of the club's events and programs - including two Blood Drives, an Art Salon Series, Candidates' Night and a Holiday Open House - are open to the public each year. Its Julia Morgan-designed clubhouse is a center for many community functions and is a popular rental site for weddings and receptions. Members enthusiastically support two nonprofit organizations of the club, the SWC Scholarship Recognition Fund and the SWC Preservation Society. All proceeds of *Cooking With a View* will go toward the preservation of the clubhouse.

SAUSALITO
Cooking with a View

By the Sausalito Woman's Club

Additional copies may be obtained at the cost of $25.00, plus $4.00 postage and handling for first book ($1.50 each additional book shipped to same address).
California residents add $1.80 sales tax, each book.

Send to:

Sausalito Woman's Club
P.O. Box 733
Sausalito, CA 94966

First Printing, January 2000
Second Printing, April 2002

ISBN: 0-9715892-0-8

WIMMER
C O O K B O O K S
ConsolidatedGraphics
1-800-548-2537

The Spirit of the
Sausalito Woman's Club

When the rasp of saws shattered the quiet of her Sausalito hillside home, that banner day in 1911, Ella Wood raced out into Bulkley Avenue. There, where a stand of stately cypress trees had shaded her walks on many a pleasant afternoon, lay a mountain of sawed-off stumps and severed branches, the work of woodcutters already moving on to the few remaining victims. Immediately energized, Ella raced through the streets, arousing her neighbors to the emergency. Ten women answered her call, joining hands to circle the last tree remaining, while others enlisted the aid of the town clerk to halt its destruction. On that day the spirit of the Sausalito Woman's Club was born.

Three of the women - Elizabeth Shoobert, Lydia Sperry, and Nellie Story - made up their minds that the saving of what came to be known as "The Founders' Tree" should signal the beginning of a club "of civic force to save the beauty of our hillsides." Their resolve reflected a general attitude emerging at the turn of the century that, if women were to have a voice at all, they would need to join together in organizations to be heard. By April 3, 32 women had signed the club constitution and paid their dues. Eventually they formulated the mission statement that prevails to this day:

"The Purpose of the Sausalito Woman's Club shall be to preserve the beauty of Sausalito, to aid through organized effort such worthy causes as may enlist its sympathies and to create a center of thought and action among the people for the promotion of whatever tends for the best interest of this town and of the state."

By 1918 the Sausalito Woman's Club had moved into the home it now occupies on Central Avenue. The graceful redwood structure had risen on land donated in the memory of one of its early members, Grace McGregor Robbins, and reflected the vision of the club founders and of their renowned architect. They had chosen Julia Morgan, the first woman to receive a California architect's license, to execute and supervise the original design and subsequent additions. The beautiful clubhouse would be named Sausalito Landmark #1 almost sixty years later, and would be placed on the National Register of Historic Places in 1993.

Throughout the years the Sausalito Woman's Club has remained true to its mission statement, consistently rallying its members to action on a variety of community issues related to civics, education, and conservation. Its 300 members continue to honor their founders on the third Thursday of March each year, with a gala luncheon and variety show - the Jinks. Here, past and present join to celebrate the shared community spirit that remains as vital today as it was in 1911.

By Jacqueline Kudler

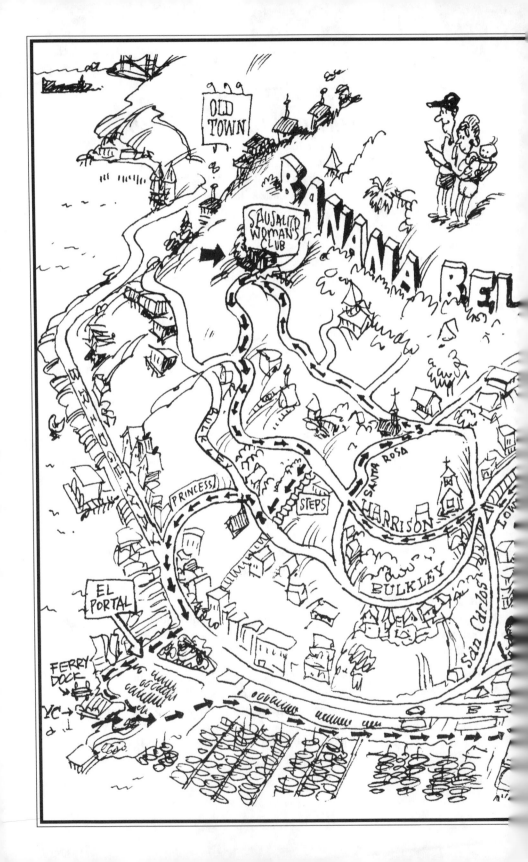

·SAUSALITO·AF!!T·

Sausalito Woman's Club Centennial Walk

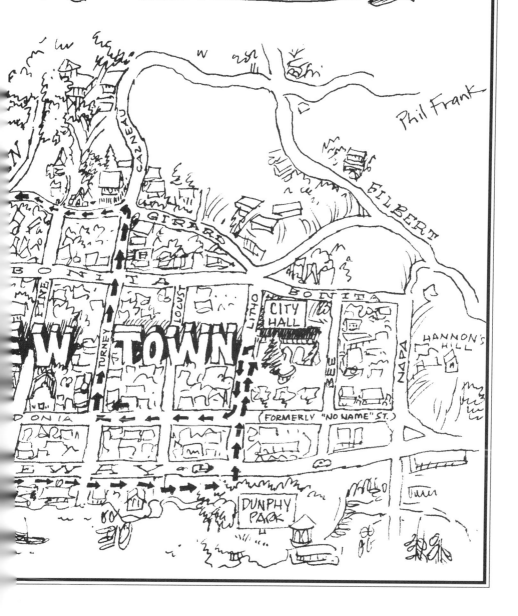

Phil Frank

W TOWN

CITY HALL

HANNON'S HILL

(FORMERLY "NO NAME" ST.)

DUNPHY PARK

Cookbook Committee

Chair .... Agnes D. Kaprielian

Vice-Chairs .... Barbara Lockhart
                       Noel Norton

Committee Members

Adrianne Burton   Marty Kortebein
Mary Ann Dietrich   Heidi Snowden
Carol Fraser   Betsy Stafford
Becky Holbrook

Creative Writers

Pat & Tim Boddy   Hope McCrum
Susan Frank   Gunvor Ross
Marty Kortebein   Bea Seidler
Jacqueline Kudler   Shelby Van Meter

Art Work

Cover and Divider Page Watercolors .... Ruth Alexander Stewart

Additional Art Work .... Phil Frank
                                                    Scottie Libberton
                                                    Heidi Snowden
                                                    Alice Merrill
                                                    Ruth Alexander Stewart

Word Processing

Kim Huff   Noel Norton

Editing

Mary Ann Dietrich   Barbara Lockhart
Marty Kortebein   Betsy Stafford
Jacqueline Kudler

Sales and Distribution

Lucinda Chriss   Ellen Cunningham
Agnes Kaprielian   Wera Musaus

Acknowledgments

The members of the Sausalito Woman's Club have played an important and ongoing role in the development of this cookbook. Recipes have been submitted by members who have used them throughout their lives, prepared them for various Club events, or tested new ones on their willing family and friends. Text has been included that describes the life, times and events in Sausalito, a place we call "Paradise."

Angels

Special thanks are extended to the Angels who came through with much appreciated grants and assistance to make this book a reality.

Mike Stone,
Mollie Stone's Markets

Merv Regan,
Sausalito Chamber of Commerce

Nora Smith,
WestAmerica Bank

Herbie Weiner,
Sausalito Automotive

Tim McDonnell,
Spinnaker Restaurant

Luz-Mary and Steve Harris

Agnes and Leonard Kaprielian

Bruce Kortebein

Barbara and Wood Lockhart

Betsy and Bob Stafford

Patricia Zuch

Jerry Anne DiVecchio,
Senior Food Editor, *Sunset Magazine*

A heartfelt "Thank You" to Jerry Anne DiVecchio for a wonderful cooking lesson presented at the Sausalito Woman's Club celebrating the completion of this cookbook.

Recipe Contributors

Jeniffer Anton
Stan Anton
Ann Arnott
Helen Arthur
Judy Belding
Amy Belser
Betty Ann Berkman
Myra Berkowitz
Barbara Blakely
Tim Boddy
Inez Brock
Adrianne Burton
Kirke Byers
Betty Anne Carlin
Janet Chapman
Gertude Churchill
Dianne Chute
Cindy Cione
Vera Clouette
DeAnne Cole
Diane Connor
Thelma Constantinidis
Eleanor Cruikshank
Nancy Curran
Nancy DeBruyn
Mary Ann Dietrich
Anne Dinelli
Jerry Anne DiVecchio
Lillian Donald
Dorothy Dumas
Shirley Elkington
Laurice Evans
Kelny Farber
Linda Felt
Linda Fotsch
Carol Fraser
Ellen Fuerst
Margot Gergus
Peg Gildersleeve

Tyke Glaser
Anne Grace
Holland Gray
Mary Ann Griller
Peggy Hall
Diane Hansen
Kathleen Hecker
Jane Hirsch
Sue Hock
Becky Holbrook
Barbara Holmes
Nikki Johnson
Janet Kaplan
Agnes Kaprielian
Marie Kearns
Marty Kortebein
Jacqueline Kudler
Vicki Larsen
Jeane Lapkin
Scottie Libberton
Janette Lischeske
James Liu
Mickie Lloyd
Barbara Lockhart
Kathryn Maas
Dorothy MacLaird
Dina Maggiora
Elizabeth McBride
Hope McCrum
Ted McCrum
Terry McFeely
Andrea McManus-Stare
Charlotte Mitchell
Deborah Moore
Cis Muldoon
Wera Musaus
Noel Norton
Linda Neilsen
Linda Ojeda

Maryann Pacula
Helen Parkman
Bonnie Penprase
Saga Perry
Kate Powell
Carole Raisbeck
Rick Reide
Elizabeth Redor
Barbara Rich
Karen Roark
Susan Roegiers
Sharon Rolfes
Gunvor Ross
Sylvia Ruby
Rosemary Russell
Margery Schindler
Mabrey Scott
Rosemary Seal
Bea Seidler
Nora Smith
Susan Smith
Heidi Snowden
Betsy Stafford
Deborah Stephenson
Don Stewart
Ruth Stewart
Denise Stine
Lucy Suckle
Barbara Sutak
Nancie Tatum
Marimar Torres
Nancy Trenner
Shelby Van Meter
Jan Wahl
Eugenie Waldteufel
Julie Warren
Margaret Wheaton
Sandra Macleod White
Busaba Williams
Babette Wurtz

Table of Contents

Recipe Testers

These wonderful women tested recipes on their unsuspecting families and friends. We are grateful to them for their generous contributions and evaluations.

Dianne Andrews
Jeniffer Anton
Ann Arnott
Gerry Beers
Toni Boynton
Michele Cambron
Julie Carlson
Beverly Christensen
Cindi Cione
Karen Cleary
DeAnne Cole
Nancy DeBruyn
Mary Ann Dietrich
Loren Gordon
Jan Gould
Mary Henry de Tessan
Becky Holbrook
Kim Huff
Agnes Kaprielian
Marty Kortebein
Mickie Lloyd
Barbara Lockhart

Roberta Maloy
Charlotte Mastrangelo
Elizabeth McBride
Jean McCardle
Hope McCrum
Terry McFeely
Noel Norton
Jean Patterson
Peggy Ann Plumley
Barbara Rich
Gunvor Ross
Nancy Sheppard
Heidi Snowden
Jean Spaulding
Betsy Stafford
Linda Swanson
Shelby Van Meter
Julie Warren
Katherine Whittaker
Arliss Willis
Nancy Wolf

Appetizers
and Beverages

Mt. Tamalpais
from Sausalito

Alex

The Sausalito Springs

"I think someone forgot to turn off a faucet. I heard water running all night." The worried look on our houseguest's face was unmistakable. His concern was timely: we were in the middle of a dry year, and saving water was essential.

"Don't worry about it," I said. "What you hear is our neighbor's waterfall. That water doesn't go to waste - it's recycled, and it's fed by a spring that runs clear and sweet, even in years of drought."

Long before Sausalito was developed, fresh water springs and streams were abundant here, creating watering holes and lush grazing for a rich variety of wildlife. Today five springs remain among the rolling hills.

Sausalito's fresh water has played a pivotal role in our history. In 1822 an English sailor, William A. Richardson, arrived in San Francisco. By 1827 he had a profitable business of selling water to ships anchored off Sausalito, some of them whaling ships. A ship's crew would throw the empty casks overboard, tie them together, tow them ashore, lug them up the hillside, fill them, and then roll them back down. Longboats hauled them out to the waiting ship. Later Captain Richardson built flumes to carry the water to the beach. Richardson's Bay was named in honor of this early pioneer.

After the 1906 earthquake Sausalito springs supplied water to San Francisco. Throughout dry spells homeowners blessed with access to the five remaining springs have been able to maintain beautiful, lush gardens. How lucky we are to live with the illusion of cascading mountain streams right outside our front doors!

By Gunvor Sande Ross

Chili Cheese Dip

Makes about 4 cups.

1   12-ounce jar mild green chili salsa
12   ounces cheddar cheese, grated
1   6-ounce can sliced olives
3   green onions, thinly sliced
Tortilla chips

In a very heavy saucepan heat salsa and add cheese gradually until well blended. Then add olives. Put in serving dish and garnish with green onions. Serve warm with chips.

Aïoli

For garlic lovers.

Makes about 2 cups.

2   **egg yolks**
1   **rounded teaspoon Dijon mustard**
1   **teaspoon lemon juice or vinegar**
1¼   **cups vegetable oil**
4-5   **large cloves garlic**
Crudités

In the bowl of a food processor put egg yolks, mustard, lemon juice, 1 tablespoon vegetable oil and garlic. Turn on the machine, and add oil very slowly, almost drop by drop, through the feed tube, until mixture has thickened. The remaining oil can be added a little faster. Process until desired consistency. Serve with selection of fresh vegetables, or serve in small mortar as a substitute for butter with French bread. Use the pestle instead of a knife to spread.

Eggplant Dip

Makes 2 to 3 cups.

2½-3 **pounds eggplant**

5 **tablespoons fresh lemon juice**

1 **tablespoon chopped garlic**

1 **teaspoon sea salt**

⅛ **teaspoon black or white pepper**

⅔ **cup olive oil**

½ **cup plain yogurt**

¼ **cup cilantro, chopped**

To prepare eggplant in microwave, pierce with a knife, and cook one at a time on high for 7 to 9 minutes, depending on size, until very soft. Peel and proceed with recipe. If no microwave is available, roast eggplants over an open flame or on a barbecue until the skin blisters, adjusting the heat so that the eggplants are soft all the way through by the time the entire surface is blistered. Cool in refrigerator. (This can be done the night before.) Peel and discard skins and stems.

Puree eggplant in a food processor until smooth in 2 to 3 batches. Add lemon juice, garlic, salt and pepper. Slowly add olive oil. Remove to a bowl and stir in the yogurt and cilantro. Adjust seasoning to taste. Refrigerate and enjoy as a dip for fresh or roasted vegetables, with pita bread or in a sandwich.

Southeast Asian Peanut Dip

Flavor is hot but very good.

Makes about 1½ cups.

2	teaspoons peanut or salad oil
2	teaspoons butter
1	medium onion, chopped
3	cloves garlic, minced
1	teaspoon molasses or honey
¼	cup hot water
3	heaping tablespoons crunchy peanut butter
4	tablespoons lime juice
1	teaspoon Tabasco sauce
1	tablespoon brown sugar
1	tablespoon soy sauce

Heat oil and butter, and stir fry onions and garlic until golden. Remove and drain on paper towels. Dissolve molasses in hot water. Add peanut butter to hot pan, then molasses mixture and lime juice. Bring to a boil. Remove pan from heat and add rest of ingredients. Stir in onions and garlic. Serve as dipping sauce for fresh vegetables. Also good as sauce for broiled meats or over salads.

Hot Artichoke and Green Chili Spread

Makes about 1¼ cups.

1   **14-ounce can artichoke hearts, drained and finely chopped**
1   **4-ounce can mild, chopped green chiles**
¾   **cup mayonnaise**
6-8 **ounces Parmesan cheese, freshly grated**
Cayenne pepper to taste
Tabasco sauce to taste
Salt to taste

Mix all ingredients thoroughly. Spoon into ovenproof container and bake at 350 degrees for 20 minutes. Serve with plain crackers or sliced baguettes.

Smoked Salmon Cheese Roll

Makes about 3 cups.

1   **pound cream cheese, room temperature**
3   **tablespoons capers**
3   **tablespoons finely chopped Bermuda onion**
1   **tomato, seeded and chopped**
6   **ounces smoked salmon, chopped**
1   **teaspoon fresh lemon juice**
Salt to taste
1   **cup chopped fresh parsley**

Carefully combine all ingredients except parsley. Shape mixture into log and chill.

Roll log in parsley to coat. Serve with mini-bagels or crackers.

Camembert Mold

Makes about 2 cups.

½   **pound Camembert cheese**
¼   **cup sherry**
1   **cup butter, or ½ butter ½ cream cheese**
Juice of 1 lemon
1-2   cups water
Pears, sliced
Apples, sliced
White grapes
Wheat wafers

Two days before serving remove rind from cheese. If not soft enough to level in bowl, microwave a few seconds or warm slightly in oven. Pour sherry over top and refrigerate overnight. The day before, drain and reserve sherry. Blend the butter and Camembert. Using an electric beater, slowly add sherry. Turn into 1½ cup mold and refrigerate. Unmold 1 hour before serving.

Mix together lemon juice and water. Dip fruit slices in mixture and drain in colander. Arrange cheese with fruit and crackers.

Carrot Cheese Roll
Low fat and delicious!

Makes about 1 cup.

> **2 medium carrots, finely shredded**
> **4 ounces reduced-calorie, soft-style cream cheese**
> **3 tablespoons grated Parmesan cheese**
> **¼ teaspoon fines herbes**
> **¼ cup Grape Nuts cereal**
> **1 cucumber, sliced**
> **Low-fat crackers**

In a small mixing bowl stir together carrots, cream cheese, Parmesan cheese and fines herbes. Cover and chill cheese mixture for at least 1 hour or overnight.

Just before serving, slightly crush Grape Nuts cereal. Shape cheese mixture into a 7-inch long log. Then roll cheese log in the crushed cereal to coat evenly.

Serve with sliced cucumbers or crackers or both.

Baked Garlic Appetizer

Makes about 3½ cups.

4	**large garlic heads, unpeeled**
2½	**tablespoons butter, thinly sliced**
¼	**cup olive oil**
2-2½	**cups chicken broth**
2	**cups sun-dried tomatoes**
¾	**tablespoon dried fines herbes**
	Freshly ground pepper
6	**ounces goat cheese, sliced**
	Fresh basil leaves
1	**large loaf Italian bread, sliced**

Preheat oven to 375 degrees. Slice ¼ inch off tops of garlic heads (opposite root end). Remove any loose outer papery skin. Place garlic, cut side up, in medium baking dish. Arrange butter slices evenly over garlic. Pour oil over garlic. Add 2 cups broth to dish. Arrange sun-dried tomatoes around garlic. Sprinkle with fines herbes. Season with pepper. Bake until garlic and sun-dried tomatoes are tender. Baste with broth every 15 minutes, adding more broth if necessary to maintain some sauce in pan. Bake about one hour, 15 minutes.

Arrange goat cheese around garlic and continue baking until cheese is almost melted about 10 minutes. Garnish with basil. Serve with Italian bread.

Mousseline of Chicken Livers

Makes about 4 cups.

6   ounces chicken livers
Salt and pepper
4   whole eggs
2   cups whipping cream

TOPPING
1   tablespoon chopped shallots
2   tablespoons red wine vinegar
1   cup white wine
1   cup port wine
4   tablespoons crème fraîche
3   tablespoons plus 1 teaspoon sweet butter

Clean the livers and chop them in the food processor. Add salt and pepper. Then add the eggs. While this preparation is mixing, add the whipping cream, little by little. Put the resulting mixture through a sieve. Butter a mold, or individual molds and spoon in the liver mixture. Place mold or molds in a pan of water and bake at 350 degrees for 45 minutes.

For the topping cook the shallots, white wine, red wine vinegar and port wine in heavy saucepan. When all the liquid has evaporated, add the crème fraîche. Then beat in the sweet butter. Put all these ingredients through a sieve and spread over the mousseline. Serve with toast.

Mushrooms, truffles, capers or black olives can be substituted for or used with shallots.

Sun-Dried Tomato and Pesto Torte

A pretty red and green treat for the holidays.

Makes about 2 cups.

1	**cup butter, softened**
½	**pound cream cheese, softened**
½	**cup sun-dried tomato pesto**
¼	**cup basil pesto**
⅓	**cup toasted pine nuts**

Mix together equal parts butter and cream cheese. Moisten and wring dry 2 large squares of cheesecloth. Smoothly line a 5-to 6-cup mold, draping excess cloth over rim (a straight-sided bowl or small soufflé pan works best). Carefully spoon in ⅓ of cream cheese mixture and smooth to edges. Spoon on a layer of ¼ cup tomato pesto and smooth out. Spoon another ⅓ cream cheese mixture and smooth to edges. Spoon on remaining ¼ cup tomato pesto and smooth out. Finish with last ⅓ cream cheese mixture smoothed out. Fold cheesecloth over top and refrigerate until firm, about 1 to 1½ hours. Gently pull off cloth. If made ahead, cover and refrigerate for up to 5 days.

About an hour before serving place on serving platter. Cover with basil pesto. Pat on pine nuts to cover top. Surround with crostini to serve.

The unique charm of Sausalito's steep hillsides and magnificent bay views has always attracted creative individuals. The gentle pace and low cost of living along the waterfront and on the water also encouraged the growth of the artistic community.

Bulgur Wheat Balls

*Try these stuffed into pocket bread garnished with chopped
parsley and onion for a great vegetarian sandwich!*

Makes 30 balls.

2	**large white onions, chopped**
4	**tablespoons margarine or butter**
½	**cup salad oil**
2	**cups very fine bulgur**
2	**6-ounce cans tomato paste**
1-1½	**cans water (use tomato paste can)**
½	**teaspoon or less cayenne**

Salt to taste
Paprika for color

1	**bunch parsley, minced**
1	**Bermuda onion, chopped fine for garnish**

Sauté chopped onions in margarine and oil until wilted and glossy
white. Do not brown. Combine onion and all the remaining ingredients except parsley in a bowl and knead well. About ½ cup of the
parsley may be added, if desired. Refrigerate 20 to 40 minutes, or as
long as overnight. Shape into small balls. Arrange on serving platter.
Sprinkle with more chopped parsley and Bermuda onion. Can be
prepared several days ahead and stored in an airtight container until
ready to shape, garnish and serve.

Sweet Potato Chips

Makes as many chips as you need.

Sweet potatoes
Salt

Preheat oven to 375 degrees. Leaving skin on, thinly slice potatoes
about ⅛-inch thick. Arrange on oiled cookie sheet. Bake for 10 to 15
minutes until the edges curl and slices brown slightly. Salt, if desired.

Oriental Chicken Wings

These are always the first appetizers to disappear.

Serves 4 to 6.

- **24 chicken wings, tips removed**
- **1 cup cornstarch**
- **2 eggs, beaten**
- **½ teaspoon salt**
- **Dash of garlic salt**
- **½ cup milk**
- **4 cups cooking oil**

ORIENTAL SAUCE
- **1 cup sugar**
- **¼ cup water**
- **½ cup rice vinegar**
- **1 teaspoon soy sauce**
- **1 tablespoon catsup**

Cut the wings at the joint. Using upper portion of wing, scrape and push meat to end of bone so that each piece resembles a small drumstick. In a mixing bowl combine cornstarch, eggs, salt, garlic salt and milk. Dip each chicken piece in batter, coating completely. Heat cooking oil at least 1-inch deep in a skillet or wok over moderate-high heat. Cook 6 or 7 batter coated pieces at a time for 5 to 6 minutes, turning often until lightly browned. Remove from fat and set aside to drain on paper towels.

In a small saucepan combine sugar, water, vinegar, soy sauce and catsup. Place over medium heat, stirring until sugar is dissolved about 7 to 10 minutes. Remove from heat. Dip each piece in Oriental Sauce. Place in a single layer in a shallow baking pan. Pour the remaining sauce over chicken and bake in a preheated oven at 350 degrees for 30 minutes. Baste and turn the chicken pieces as they are heating. Serve warm or cold.

Chicken Teriyaki
with Thai Peanut Sauce

The peanut sauce is also delicious on raw vegetables, rice, pork, etc.

Makes 20 skewers.

20   boneless chicken thighs

Teriyaki sauce

**20   wooden skewers, presoaked in water for
30 minutes**

THAI PEANUT SAUCE

2   cups chunky peanut butter

½   cup brown sugar

¼   cup soy sauce

2   teaspoons garlic powder

2   teaspoons ground cumin

2   teaspoons ground cardamom

Dash Tabasco sauce

1   cup hot tea

Cut each thigh into 4 chunks. Marinate in teriyaki sauce. Thread 4 pieces chicken onto each skewer. Bake at 350 degrees for about 7 or 8 minutes per side or until done.

Mix together peanut butter, brown sugar, soy sauce, garlic powder, cumin, cardamom, Tabasco and tea. Serve with skewered chicken.

Cheese Straws

Makes 60 straws.

- **1   cup flour**
- **½   teaspoon salt**
- **¼   teaspoon dry mustard**
- **⅛   teaspoon cayenne pepper**
- **⅓   cup butter, room temperature**
- **1   cup grated sharp cheddar cheese**
- **1½   tablespoons ice water**

Sift flour, salt, mustard and cayenne together. Blend in butter, cheese and ice water. Shape into a ball. On a lightly floured pastry board roll dough out into a rectangular shape. Cut into strips 3-inches x ½-inch, using either a knife or pastry wheel. Bake at 350 degrees for 14 minutes on an ungreased cookie sheet until pale brown.

Mushroom Duxelles and Brie Tartlets

Makes 18 tartlets.

- **2   ounces dried porcini mushrooms, soaked in hot water**
- **1   pound mushrooms, chopped fine**
- **2   yellow onions, chopped fine**
- **Butter**
- **18   tartlet shells**
- **Brie cheese**

Chop porcini mushrooms and wring dry. Sauté all mushrooms and onions in butter over low heat until all moisture is evaporated. This can be made well ahead and frozen or refrigerated. Put a small amount in tartlet shell and place a small piece of Brie on top. Heat at 350 degrees for about 5 minutes, or until cheese is melted. Serve immediately.

Agnes' Stuffed Grape Leaves

Makes 60 appetizers.

4	large onions, finely chopped
1	cup white rice
1	cup olive oil
1	8-ounce can tomato sauce
½	cup water
¼	cup chopped parsley
3	tablespoons lemon juice
2	teaspoons dill

Salt and pepper to taste

¼	teaspoon cinnamon
¼	teaspoon allspice
¼	teaspoon cayenne
⅓	cup pine nuts, optional
60	grape leaves

Extra grape leaves or lettuce, torn

¼	cup olive oil
1½	cups water
¼	cup lemon juice

Sauté onions in olive oil until transparent. Add rice and sauté a minute or more to coat the grains of rice with oil. Add remaining ingredients through pine nuts and cook about 15 minutes.

Rinse the grape leaves and open up the bunches on a pie plate. Spread 1 leaf at a time on a plate. Pinch off the stem; put 1 tablespoon of rice mixture on the leaf. Fold sides in and roll the leaf up. Place seam side down in a 5-quart pan that has been lined on the bottom with torn grape or lettuce leaves to prevent them from sticking.

Mix the ¼ cup olive oil with the water and lemon juice, and pour over the grape leaves. Cover with more torn grape or lettuce leaves to prevent the tops from turning black. Place an inverted plate on top to keep them from floating while cooking. Bring to a boil and simmer

Agnes' Stuffed Grape Leaves (continued)

until tender and water is almost absorbed, about 30 to 40 minutes. Cool and leave in pot. Don't refrigerate until next day. Serve chilled.

These may also be wrapped, refrigerated, but not cooked until 2 days before they are to be served. They can also be wrapped and frozen, defrosted and cooked 2 days before they are needed. This stuffing is very versatile and can be used to make small stuffed egg-plants, stuffed cabbage leaves or stuffed tomatoes. These vegetables do not have to be covered on top. They may be simmered on top of the stove or baked in a 350 degree oven for 50 minutes. This is a wonderful meatless entrée and can be served warm or at room temperature.

Artichoke Frittata

Makes 36 bite-sized pieces.

2   **6-ounce jars marinated artichoke hearts**
3   **green onions, chopped**
1   **clove garlic, mashed**
4   **eggs**
6   **soda crackers, crumbled**
Salt and pepper to taste
½   **pound sharp cheddar cheese, grated**
2   **tablespoons chopped parsley**
¼   **cup Parmesan cheese**

Drain marinade from the artichokes into a skillet. Chop the artichokes and set aside. Add onions and garlic to skillet. Sauté until onions are limp. In a bowl beat eggs with wire whisk. Add soda crackers, salt and pepper. Stir in cheese, parsley, artichokes and onion mixture. Pour mixture into a buttered 8-inch x 8-inch pan. Sprinkle with Parmesan cheese. Bake at 325 degrees for 35 to 40 minutes until set. Let cool in pan, then cut into bite-sized squares. Can be served warm or cold.

Hedda Hopper's
Spill Your Guts Curried Nuts

*Hedda would serve these with large amounts of alcohol,
and the stars would eventually spill their stories.*

Makes 2 cups.

¼   **cup olive oil**
1   **tablespoon curry powder**
1   **tablespoon Worcestershire sauce**
⅛   **teaspoon cayenne**
2   **cups mixed nuts**

Heat olive oil, curry powder, Worcestershire and cayenne in skillet.
Add nuts and stir until coated well. Line a baking pan with brown or
parchment paper. Pour on nuts and bake at 300 degrees for about
10 minutes. Serve warm nuts with your favorite alcoholic drink.

Oysters Bingo

This recipe is a favorite at a local restaurant.

Serves 1 to 2.

1	**bunch spinach**
	Olive oil
	Salt and pepper
¾	**cup mayonnaise**
1	**tablespoon chopped garlic**
2	**tablespoons grated Asiago cheese**
1	**tablespoon fresh lemon juice**
1	**tablespoon brandy**
	Salt and pepper to taste
6	**oysters on the half shell**
	Lemon wedge

Sauté 1 bunch of spinach in olive oil and season with salt and pepper. Combine mayonnaise, garlic, Asiago cheese, lemon juice, brandy, salt and pepper. Place 2 tablespoons sautéed spinach under each oyster and top with 1 tablespoon of sauce.

Heat oysters in a shallow baking pan at 400 degrees for 5 minutes. Then place under hot broiler until sauce is golden brown. Serve with a lemon wedge. This recipe is easily doubled.

Many of the major streets of Sausalito wind along the vertical length of the hillsides. Stairways intersect the streets at various intervals, allowing the many walkers in this town to easily traverse the hills from top to bottom. Many of the stairways, landscaped by both nature and the occupants of the houses along the stairs, offer glimpses into the residential character of the neighborhoods.

Prawns with Lime Mayonnaise

Serves 8 to 10.

2   **cups mayonnaise**
¼   **cup Dijon mustard**
¼   **cup fresh lime juice**
2   **tablespoons Worcestershire sauce**
4   **teaspoons Tabasco sauce**
1   **teaspoon grated lime peel**
¼   **teaspoon cayenne pepper**
Salt and pepper
40   **large prawns, shelled, deveined and cooked**
Lime wedges

Mix together mayonnaise, mustard, lime juice, Worcestershire, Tabasco, grated lime peel, cayenne pepper, salt and pepper in a small bowl. Cover and refrigerate 2 days to allow flavors to mellow. Top mayonnaise with grated peel and cayenne. Place bowl in center of platter. Surround with prawns and lime wedges.

In the water off Bridgeway a sculpted sea lion greets Sausalito visitors. Originally made in cement by sculptor Al Sybrian, it was recast in bronze in 1966, thanks to the Sausalito Foundation.

Smoked Salmon on Potato Pancake

Serves 4.

3	peeled russet potatoes
2	leeks, white parts very finely shredded
1	clove garlic, mashed
2	tablespoons flour
2	eggs

Salt and pepper to taste
Sour cream
Chopped chives

12	slices of smoked salmon

Finely shred potatoes and squeeze dry. Add leeks, garlic, flour, eggs, salt and pepper and mix thoroughly. Cover and let stand for 30 minutes. On hot, oiled griddle, drop ½ cup of mixture and flatten until thin, browning well on both sides. Cook 3 more pancakes. Spread small amount of sour cream and chopped chives on each pancake and top each with 3 salmon slices. Serve warm.

Gravlax with Spicy Cucumbers, Red Onions, Mustard-Dill Sauce and Wasabi Cream Sauce

*This recipe was given to us at a demonstration
by the chef of one of our local restaurants.*

Serves 8.

2	pounds fillet of salmon with skin
½	cup kosher salt
½	cup sugar
¼	cup whole mustard seeds, toasted and crushed
¼	cup Italian parsley leaves
2	tablespoons Chardonnay

Prepare salmon 3 to 4 days in advance of use. Remove all small bones from fillet of salmon. Mix salt, sugar and mustard seed. Rub mixture on both sides of the fillet. Crush Italian parsley with hands and cover the flesh side of fillet with the herb. Sprinkle with Chardonnay. Wrap fish carefully in cheesecloth. Place in pan large enough to allow for some expansion. Put a flat bottomed pan with a weight on top of fish. Refrigerate 3 to 4 days.

When ready to serve brush salt and herb mixture off fish. Slice diagonally as thin as possible. Arrange salmon on a plate with cucumber and onions. Garnish with Italian parsley. Serve with thin slices of baguette.

SPICY CUCUMBERS

2	cucumbers
1	cup rice wine vinegar
1	tablespoon chili oil
1	tablespoon kosher salt

Pinch of crushed chiles

Pinch of black pepper

Peel cucumbers and cut in half lengthwise. Take seeds out. Slice cucumber thinly at an angle. Mix remaining ingredients and toss with cucumber slices.

Gravlax (continued)

MARINATED RED ONIONS
2-3   **cups rice wine vinegar**
1   **tablespoon sugar**
1   **tablespoon Kosher salt**
2   **red onions, thinly sliced**

Mix vinegar, sugar and salt until dissolved. Soak onions in the mixture overnight.

Here are some other good sauces to serve with gravlax.

MUSTARD-DILL SAUCE
2   **tablespoons Dijon mustard**
1   **tablespoon sugar**
1   **egg yolk**
2   **tablespoons vinegar**
½   **cup olive oil**
Chopped dill
Salt and white pepper

Mix mustard, sugar, egg yolk and vinegar in food processor. Slowly add oil. When thickened to desired consistency, add dill, salt and pepper. If you are uncomfortable using uncooked egg yolks, this recipe is not for you.

WASABI CREAM
½   **cup crème fraîche**
½   **cup wasabi paste**

Mix equal amounts of ingredients until smooth. Use sparingly as this is very hot.

Eggless Nog

Makes about 24 servings.

½   **gallon French vanilla ice cream**
1   **pint whipping cream, whipped**
1   **pint rum**
½   **pint brandy**

Let ice cream soften in a punch bowl. Fold in whipped cream. Add rum and brandy. Serve in punch cups.

Sangría

Serves 4 to 6.

½   **lemon, cut into ¼-inch slices**
½   **orange, cut into ¼-inch slices**
½   **apple, cut into thin wedges**
¼-½   **cup superfine sugar**
1   **bottle (750 ml.) dry red wine**
¼   **cup brandy**
12-24   **ounces club soda, chilled**

Combine lemon, orange and apples slices with ¼ cup sugar in a large pitcher. Pour in the wine and brandy and stir until well mixed. Taste. If you prefer the sangría sweeter, add up to ¼ cup more sugar.

Refrigerate for at least 1 hour or until thoroughly chilled. Just before serving, pour in chilled soda to taste, adding up to 24 ounces of soda. Stir again and serve at once in chilled wine glasses.

Champagne and Rum Tropical Punch

Makes about 20 punch cups.

4   **cups apricot nectar**
4   **cups pineapple juice**
4   **cups guava nectar**
2   **cups light rum**
     Ice cubes or fancy ice mold
6   **cups chilled champagne or sparkling wine**

Mix apricot nectar, pineapple juice, guava nectar and light rum in a large pitcher or bowl. Cover and refrigerate until cold. Can be prepared 1 day ahead. For a festive touch freeze nonpoisonous flowers in ice mold. When ready to serve, place ice in punch bowl. Pour juice mixture over. Add champagne. Ladle into cups and serve.

Party Punch

This is a nonalcoholic version.

Makes 50 servings.

4   **6-ounce cans frozen lemonade concentrate**
4   **6-ounce cans frozen pineapple juice concentrate**
2   **juice cans water**
2   **large 1-liter bottles ginger ale**
1   **large 1-liter bottle soda water**

Defrost lemonade and pineapple juice. Add water and stir. Just before serving, pour into punch bowl and add ginger ale and soda water. Serve in punch cups.

At Christmas time use pink lemonade and add cranberry juice.

Orange Julia

A great company or special occasion breakfast or brunch drink.

Makes about 6 small cups.

1	6-ounce can of frozen orange juice
1	cup milk
1	cup water
¼-½	cup sugar
1	teaspoon vanilla
10-12	ice cubes

Put all ingredients in a blender and blend about 1 minute. Serve immediately.

Fruit Smoothie

Makes 4 cups.

1	pound of 3 of your favorite fruits, frozen
1	banana
1	6-ounce can frozen orange juice concentrate
1	cup milk
2-3	tablespoons yogurt

Put all ingredients in blender. Blend until smooth. Serve immediately.

Sausalito remains a colorful, diverse community with a population of 7,650 residents.

Soups
and Salads

Sausalito Potpourri

For early morning walkers, a stroll on Sausalito's waterfront can turn into a veritable feast for the senses. Amblers are treated to eye-popping vistas of the San Francisco Bay and cityscape, cries of gulls wheeling overhead, and smells emanating from the kitchens of waterfront restaurants as they rev up for the day's menus.

Already the great stock pots are bubbling, filling the morning air along Bridgeway with aromas of rich chicken broths and beefy brews. A few doors on, the unmistakable fragrance of garlic sizzling in olive oil is harbinger of the evening's cioppinos, bouillabaisses, pasta puttanescas. Turn a corner, and breakfast is sputtering on the grill of local coffee shops: thick slabs of bacon, eggs-over-easy, buttermilk flapjacks.

By the time you reach the donut shop with its spicy bouquet of sweet dough in the deep fry, you know you've met your match. Well, maybe it's not too early, after all, to sit down to a second cup of coffee and something.

By Jaqueline Kudler

Cold Avocado Soup

Cut the calories by substituting whole milk or low-fat buttermilk.

Serves 4.

1   13½-ounce can chicken broth, chilled
¼   cup lemon juice
1   tablespoon chopped fresh dill
1   large ripe avocado
1   cup heavy cream, chilled
Salt and pepper to taste
Dill sprigs for garnish

Strain chicken broth to remove any congealed fat. Place broth, lemon juice and dill in blender. Peel and pit avocado, and cut into chunks. Place in blender and puree until smooth. Pour puree into a bowl and gradually stir in cream until desired consistency. Adjust seasoning. Chill. To serve garnish soup with dill sprigs.

Variations:

Add ½ cup bay shrimp or Dungeness crabmeat.
Add 1½ teaspoons curry powder.
Add ¼ cup tequila and sprinkle fresh cilantro on top and decorate with crisp corn tortilla strips.

After the Sacramento fire of 1852 many Sausalito structures were dismantled and sold up the river for lumber to rebuild the valley metropolis.

Cold Beet Soup

Serves 4 to 6.

1	**pound fresh beets**
⅓	**cup cooking liquid, from beets**
1	**15-ounce can beef consommé, undiluted**
2	**cups buttermilk**
¼	**cup brown sugar**
2	**tablespoons fresh lemon juice**

Salt and pepper

Scrub beets well. Boil in water or steam until tender. Peel beets. Using a blender, puree beets and cooking liquid. Add consommé, buttermilk, brown sugar, and blend thoroughly. Add lemon juice, salt and pepper to taste. Mix well, cover and chill.

For an easy and fast variation, omit fresh beets and cooking liquid. Use instead one 15-ounce can julienned beets with liquid.

Gazpacho

Serve as a first course to accompany barbecued beef, lamb or chicken.

Serves 8.

³⁄₄	cup onions, coarsely chopped
³⁄₄	teaspoon garlic, minced
1	large green pepper, diced
3	large or 4 medium tomatoes, peeled, seeded and diced
2½	teaspoons salt
1	teaspoon paprika
½	teaspoon sugar
¼	teaspoon black pepper
⅓	cup olive oil
½	cup lemon juice
2	cups tomato juice
2	tablespoons sherry
½	cup cucumber, chopped
2	tablespoons chives, snipped

In a very large bowl combine the onions, garlic, green pepper, tomatoes, salt, paprika, sugar and black pepper. Stir in the oil, lemon juice, tomato juice and sherry. Chill 4 to 6 hours. (Can be made the day before.) Just before serving fold in cucumbers. Garnish with chives.

For variety add 1 cup crabmeat or shrimp.

Chilled Curried Zucchini Soup

Serves 8.

2	pounds zucchini, chopped
1	cup green onions, sliced thin
6	tablespoons butter
1	tablespoon ground cumin
1	tablespoon curry
2	cups chicken broth
3	cups buttermilk

Salt and white pepper to taste

In a large saucepan, sweat zucchini and green onions in butter over medium heat, covered, for 15 minutes. Stir in cumin and curry and cook for 2 minutes. Stir in chicken broth. Puree mixture in blender or food processor. Transfer to a bowl and add buttermilk. Season to taste. Chill at least 4 hours. Thin with additional broth or buttermilk, if needed. To serve garnish with chopped chives.

Garlic Soup

Serves 6.

14	large cloves garlic, minced
2	tablespoons butter
2	tablespoons minced parsley
1	tablespoon flour
8	cups beef broth
¼	teaspoon freshly ground pepper
6	egg yolks, beaten

In heavy saucepan over low heat, brown garlic lightly in butter with minced parsley, stirring constantly so as not to burn. Add flour and stir until slightly browned. Add broth and pepper. Simmer at least 30 minutes to 1 hour. Just before serving, turn off heat and slowly add egg yolks, stirring constantly. Serve at once.

Beef Goulash Soup

A hearty, stick-to-your-ribs soup that's a meal in itself. Make a day ahead for greater flavor. Great with home-baked bread and salad.

Serves 6 to 8.

2	onions, chopped
2	cloves garlic, minced
1½	pounds beef, cut in 1-inch cubes
¼	cup oil
2	tablespoons paprika
1	teaspoon salt
¼	teaspoon pepper
2	tablespoons flour
5	cups hot water
⅓	cup red wine vinegar
1	bay leaf
1	10¾-ounce can condensed beef broth
¼	cup tomato paste
2	teaspoons Worcestershire sauce
2	potatoes, cubed
2	carrots, cubed
2	zucchini, cubed
	Sour cream

In a 6-quart dutch oven, heat oil over medium-high heat. Sauté garlic and onion for about 5 minutes or until tender. Add beef cubes to sautéed onion mixture, and brown over high heat for about 10 minutes. Stir in paprika, salt and pepper. Sprinkle flour over beef mixture and stir until well blended. Gradually stir in hot water, then vinegar. Add bay leaf. Bring mixture to a boil, stirring until it thickens slightly. Lower heat and cover. Simmer for about 1½ hours, stirring occasionally.

Stir together beef broth, tomato paste and Worcestershire sauce. Add to beef mixture, along with potatoes and carrots. Cover and simmer for 15 minutes. Add zucchini; continue to simmer for 30 minutes or until vegetables are done. Top each serving with a spoonful of sour cream.

Borscht

Makes 4 to 5 servings.

1½	cups thinly sliced potato
1	cup thinly sliced beets
4	cups stock or water
2	tablespoons butter
1½	cups chopped onion
1	scant teaspoon caraway seeds
2	teaspoons salt
1	stalk celery, chopped
1	large sliced carrot
3	cups chopped cabbage

Black pepper

¼	teaspoon dill weed
1	tablespoon plus 1 teaspoon cider vinegar
1	tablespoon plus 1 teaspoon honey
1	cup tomato puree

Sour cream

Chopped tomato

Place potatoes, beets and stock in a saucepan and cook until tender. Save the liquid. Begin cooking the onions in butter in a large kettle. Add caraway seeds and salt. Cook until onion is translucent. Then add celery, carrots and cabbage. Add liquid from potatoes and beets. Cook covered until all the vegetables are tender. Add potatoes, beets, pepper, dill, cider vinegar, honey, and tomato puree. Cover and simmer slowly for at least 30 minutes. Taste to correct seasonings. Serve topped with sour cream, extra dill weed and chopped fresh tomatoes.

Chicken Lime Soup

Serves 6.

Olive oil cooking spray

8   **chicken thighs, boned and skinned**

6   **limes**

1½ **quarts chicken broth**

6   **cloves garlic, minced**

½   **cup diced celery**

1   **cup diced carrots**

8   **fresh mushrooms, sliced**

1½ **cups diced zucchini**

1   **14½-ounce can diced tomatoes**

½   **cup fresh cilantro, minced**

½   **cup medium salsa**

Salt and pepper

1   **package unsalted tortilla chips**

2   **cups cooked white long-grain rice**

Spray chicken thighs with olive oil and squeeze the juice of 2 limes over them in a glass casserole dish. Allow to marinate for 30 minutes or so. Grill 5 minutes to a side, or until done. Allow to cool. Shred and reserve.

Bring broth to a simmer, add garlic, celery and carrots, and simmer 15 minutes. Add zucchini and mushrooms and simmer for 5 minutes. Add the chicken, juice of remaining limes, tomatoes and simmer a few minutes. Remove from heat and stir in salsa and cilantro. Season to taste with salt and pepper. Spoon into soup bowls. Pass rice and tortilla chips in separate bowls.

Egg and Lemon Soup

Serves 4 to 6.

6	**cups chicken broth**
¼	**cup fine egg noodles, broken into small pieces**
¼	**cup white rice**
1	**teaspoon salt**
3	**eggs, room temperature**
1	**large juicy lemon, juiced with seeds removed**

Bring broth to a simmer. Carefully add the noodles, rice and salt. Cook on a low simmer until rice is soft, about 15 to 20 minutes. Beat the eggs for several minutes until light and frothy. Do not underbeat. Gradually stir in the lemon juice. Slowly spoon some of the hot broth into the egg mixture and stir vigorously. Slowly pour the egg-lemon mixture into the broth stirring briskly. If the broth is too hot, the eggs will curdle. Simmer on the lowest heat for a minute or so, then shut off flame. Serve soup hot.

When reheating the soup, never let the soup boil. Bring just to a simmer and serve at once. Soup may also be reheated in the microwave oven for approximately 2 minutes on high.

Baked Vegetable Soup

Serves 8 to 10.

2	cups diced tomatoes
2	cups cooked garbanzo beans
3-5	zucchini, sliced
1	onion, sliced
½	green pepper, diced
1½	cups dry white wine
½	teaspoon paprika
1	teaspoon salt
1	teaspoon basil
2	bay leaves
5-10	cloves garlic, minced
1¼	cups Jack cheese, grated
1	cup Romano cheese, grated
1½	cups whipping cream or whole milk

Butter a 3-quart, or larger, baking dish. Mix all ingredients, except cheeses and cream in dish. Cover and bake 1 hour at 375 degrees. Remove from oven and decrease temperature to 325 degrees. Let dish sit a few minutes, then stir in cheese and cream. Return to oven for 10 to 15 more minutes, being careful not to let it boil.

Sausalito artists and merchants donated sod and plantings to transform a former city dump into beautiful Dunphy Park. The park is a living tribute to Earl Dunphy, former mayor and longtime community contributor.

Lentil Soup

Serves 8.

1	**ham hock or shank, cut into 3 pieces**
1	**quart water**
2	**onions, thinly sliced**
3	**carrots, peeled and sliced**
2	**ribs celery, peeled and sliced**
3	**tomatoes, peeled, seeded and chopped**
2	**bay leaves**
1	**teaspoons dried thyme**
1	**teaspoon salt**
1	**12-ounce package yellow split peas or lentils, rinsed**
2	**cloves garlic, peeled and crushed**
	Salt and freshly ground pepper
1-2	**cups chicken stock, if needed**

Put ham hock or shank and water into large pot and bring to boil, then lower heat and simmer for ½ hour, skimming off any foam that comes to surface.

After ½ hour of simmering, add onions, carrots, celery, tomatoes, bay leaves, thyme, salt, peas or lentils and garlic to pot and bring to boil. At boil, cover pot and simmer soup for 1½ hours until the vegetables and lentils are tender. Remove the ham shanks and bay leaves and puree soup in the blender or pass through food mill fitted with medium blade. Return soup to pot with ham which has been removed from bone, and season to taste with salt and pepper. If necessary, thin soup a little with chicken stock. Can serve with freshly made croutons.

Do not presoak lentils or peas as they can start to ferment.

Becky's Minestrone

Serves an army, but freezes beautifully.

½	cup olive oil
2	large onions, minced
6	cloves garlic, minced
2	ham hocks
2	pounds Italian sausage, cut in ½-inch pieces
2	whole chicken breasts, boned and chopped
4	carrots, cut in ¼-inch slices
4	stalks celery, chopped
4	zucchini, chopped
1	bunch Swiss chard, chopped
1	28-ounce can tomatoes, diced
1	12-ounce package lentils
6	cups chicken broth
10	cups water
3	cubes beef bouillon
1	cup diced potatoes
2	bay leaves
1	tablespoon oregano
1	tablespoon basil
1	30-ounce can kidney beans
1	1-pound package tortellini
2	cups thin noodles

Salt and pepper
Freshly grated Parmesan cheese

Sauté onions and garlic in olive oil, until softened, about 10 minutes. Stir in ham hocks, sausage and chicken. Cook 10 minutes. Stir in carrots, celery, zucchini, and chard, and cook an additional 10 minutes. Add tomatoes, lentils, chicken broth, water, bouillon cubes, potatoes, bay leaves, oregano and basil. Simmer gently for 2½ hours. Add kidney beans, tortellini and noodles. Simmer another ½ hour. Season to taste. Serve topped with grated Parmesan cheese.

Clam Chowder

Serves 8 to 10.

1	pound bacon, cut in ½-inch dice
1	large onion, chopped
4	potatoes, cut in ½-inch cubes
1	cup chopped celery with leaves
½	teaspoon thyme
½	teaspoon paprika, optional
¼	teaspoon curry, optional
1	large bay leaf

Dash Worcestershire sauce

Salt and pepper

2	8-ounce bottles clam juice
1	14.5-ounce can chicken broth
3	6.5-ounce cans chopped clams
4	cups whole milk, divided
½	cup butter
2	tablespoons flour
¼	cup milk

Sauté bacon. Drain on paper towels. Add onion and cook 5 minutes. Add potatoes, celery, thyme, paprika, curry, bay leaf, Worcestershire, salt, pepper, clam juice and chicken broth. Simmer 30 minutes. Add clams, 3¾ cups of the milk and butter, and simmer 10 minutes. Mix flour with ¼ cup milk. Add slowly, but only use the amount needed for desired thickness. Serve at once.

Curried Corn and Tomato Soup

Serves 4 to 6.

1   **small onion, diced**
4   **cloves garlic, minced**
1   **tablespoon vegetable oil**
2   **tablespoons curry powder**
1   **teaspoon dried basil**
1   **teaspoon dried oregano**
3   **large tomatoes, diced**
3   **stalks celery, diced**
2   **cups frozen corn**
1   **large potato, peeled and diced**
3   **cups chicken stock**
Salt and pepper to taste
½   **cup coconut milk, optional**

Sauté onion and garlic in oil. Stir in curry powder, basil and oregano. Add tomatoes, celery, corn, potato and stock. Simmer gently 45 minutes, uncovered. Mash a few times with potato masher and season to taste. Add coconut milk, if desired.

Substitute a handful of pasta for the potato. Add during the final 10 minutes of cooking.

Saucelito, Saucito, Sauzalito, finally was officially spelled Sausalito by the U.S. Post Office in 1887.

Butternut Squash Bisque with Roasted Jalapeño Swirl

Serves 8.

3-3½	**pounds butternut squash**
¾	**cup butter, divided**
½	**pound leeks, cut into ½-inch slices**
½	**pound onions, chopped**
¼	**pound celery, diced**
3	**bay leaves**
6	**cilantro stalks**
6	**parsley stalks**
6	**thyme stems and leaves**
2	**quarts chicken stock**
Salt and pepper	
Cayenne pepper	
4	**jalapeño peppers**
½	**cup sour cream**
2	**cups cream**

Cut butternut squash in half and remove seeds and fiber. Place flat side down on a lightly oiled sheet pan. Bake at 300 degrees for about 45 minutes until soft to the touch. Let cool, then scoop out the flesh. Puree in food processor and set aside. Melt ½ cup butter in heavy pan. Add leeks and onions and celery. Cook a few minutes, covered, being careful not to brown. Add herbs. Stir, add stock, and bring to a boil. Simmer for 30 minutes. Add the squash puree and stir until well blended. Bring back to a boil. Season to taste with salt, pepper and cayenne. Turn off the soup. Put in a blender and puree until smooth; strain if desired.

For the swirl, cut the jalapeños in half, remove seeds and place the cut side down on an oiled sheet pan. Bake at 400 degrees for about 15 minutes until the skin turns black and wrinkles. Place in a plastic sandwich bag to sweat for about 20 to 30 minutes. Skins should

Butternut Squash Bisque (continued)

come off easily. Puree the jalapeños, adding a little liquid to get started and process until smooth. Add the puree to the sour cream until you reach your level of heat. Season with salt, pepper and a little cayenne if desired. Keep chilled.

To finish the soup, boil to reduce the cream by half, and then add to the soup base. Stirring almost all the time to avoid the soup sticking on the bottom and burning, bring to a boil. Check the seasoning and whip in remaining 4 tablespoons of the butter. Place in warm soup bowls and put a teaspoon of the jalapeño mixture in the middle and swirl to make a design. Garnish with a cilantro leaf.

Pappa al Pomodoro

This is a traditional Tuscan soup with a California twist.

Serves 8.

½ **pound stale or lightly toasted sourdough bread**
½ **cup olive oil**
6 **or more garlic cloves**
2 **sage leaves**
2 **28-ounce canned Italian style tomatoes with basil**
½ **cup chicken broth**
3 **tablespoons chopped thyme**
Garlic salt and pepper to taste
¼ **teaspoon crushed red pepper to taste**
Grated Parmesan cheese

Thinly slice the bread. Pour oil into a saucepan and add garlic and sage. Sauté until golden. Add bread, allowing it to absorb the oil for 2 minutes, stirring frequently. Blend the tomatoes in a food processor for 2 seconds. Cook 5 minutes. Add the broth and thyme. Cook over low heat for about 30 minutes, stirring occasionally. Season to taste; pass the Parmesan cheese.

Yellow Pepper Soup

Serves 6.

1	medium carrot, peeled and chopped
1	onion, chopped
1	large stalk celery, diced
¼	cup olive oil
4-6	yellow bell peppers, seeded and cut into chunks
1	pound potatoes, peeled and sliced thinly
1	10½-ounce can low-salt beef broth
3	cups water

Freshly ground pepper
Freshly made croutons, sautéed in olive oil
Freshly grated well-aged Parmesan cheese

In a large saucepan slowly sauté carrot, onion and celery in oil, stirring occasionally until all the vegetables are softened. Add peppers, potatoes, broth and water to saucepan. Bring to a boil, then reduce heat and simmer for 40 minutes or until vegetables are very soft. Puree in a blender or food processor, and add pepper to taste. Do not add salt since cheese will balance the taste. Ladle soup over croutons in serving bowls and sprinkle with cheese.

Spiced Walnut and Apple Salad

Serves 4 to 6.

1½   tablespoons butter

1   cup walnuts

⅓   cup sugar

1   teaspoon pepper

4-6 cups salad greens

4   ounces feta cheese, crumbled

1   green apple, chopped

DRESSING

1   tablespoon parsley, minced

¼   cup chopped sweet red onion

1   teaspoon oregano

1   teaspoon sugar

½   cup white wine vinegar

¾   cup olive oil

Melt butter and coat the walnuts. Mix the ⅓ cup sugar and pepper together and toss with the walnuts. Bake the coated walnuts at 350 degrees for 15 minutes, turning every 5 minutes. Put the salad greens, feta and apple in a salad bowl.

For dressing, blend parsley, onion, oregano, sugar and vinegar in a blender until smooth, then slowly add the oil. Toss salad with dressing and walnuts just before serving.

Stilton cheese and a pear can be substituted for feta cheese and apple.

Minted Citrus Salad

Serves 4.

1   head of your favorite lettuce
1   grapefruit, peeled and sectioned
2   oranges, peeled and sliced
1   avocado, peeled and sliced
2   kiwi fruit, peeled and sliced
Pomegranate seeds, if available

DRESSING

3   tablespoons mint jelly
1   tablespoon honey
1   lime, its grated rind and juice
1   tablespoon fresh mint, minced
2   tablespoons seasoned rice wine vinegar

On a bed of lettuce arrange grapefruit sections, sliced oranges, avocado slices and kiwi fruit slices. Garnish with a few kernels of pomegranate seeds. For salad dressing, melt mint jelly and mix with honey, juice of the lime, grated lime rind, fresh mint and seasoned rice wine vinegar. Pour over salads and serve.

1873 marked the start of the railroad (no longer in existence) that would link Sausalito with the North coast, and bring much needed lumber for the building boom in San Francisco.

Fiesta Salad

Serves 8.

½	**cup black beans**
½	**cup rice**
1	**8-ounce can corn**
1	**4-ounce can chopped green chili**
¼	**cup parsley, finely chopped**
¼	**cup olive oil**
2	**tablespoons cider vinegar**
2	**tablespoons mustard**
2	**cloves garlic, minced**
2	**teaspoons ground cumin**

Pour 3 cups boiling water over beans, cover and let sit for 1 hour. Drain, add fresh, cool water to cover by 1 inch and simmer until tender. Check for doneness at 30 minutes.

Cook rice following directions on package. Mix black beans, rice, corn, chili and parsley. Mix together olive oil, cider vinegar, mustard, garlic and ground cumin. Pour over bean and rice mixture. Refrigerate to blend flavors for a few hours. Serve at room temperature.

Djazar (African Carrot Salad)

Prepare the dressing the day before for a perfect blending of flavors.

Serves 8.

DRESSING
- ½ **cup olive oil**
- 6 **cloves garlic**
- 1 **teaspoon cumin**
- **Pinch cayenne pepper**
- 1 **teaspoon paprika**
- 2-3 **tablespoons lemon juice**
- 2-3 **tablespoons rice wine vinegar**
- 4 **slices fresh ginger**
- **Salt and pepper to taste**

CARROT MIXTURE
- 1 **pound baby carrots**
- 1 **red onion, thinly sliced**
- 1 **bulb fresh fennel, thinly sliced**
- ¼ **cup chopped cilantro**

For dressing, combine oil with garlic cloves in food processor. Add cumin, cayenne, paprika, lemon juice, rice wine vinegar, ginger, salt and pepper. Chill overnight.

Parboil baby carrots until al dente. Mix with red onion, fennel and cilantro. Pour dressing over carrot mixture and serve.

Marin Green Salad with Parsley Dressing

This recipe was a hit at the Marin Designers' Showcase.
It is no ordinary green salad and thus its name change.
The recipe can be reduced to serve a smaller group.

Serves 24.

1	head romaine
1	head red leaf lettuce
1	head butter lettuce
1½	pounds spring-mix lettuces
2	bunches green onions, cut in ¼-inch slices

Tear heads of lettuce into bite-size pieces. Mix with spring-mix lettuces and green onions. Toss with dressing.

Parsley Salad Dressing

2	teaspoons sugar
4	cloves garlic
1	teaspoon oregano
1	tablespoon Dijon mustard
¼	medium onion, cut up
¼	teaspoon salt
¼	teaspoon pepper
½	cup wine vinegar
1	cup parsley leaves
1½	cups olive oil

Put all ingredients in a blender and whirl away until well blended. This can be used on any sort of tossed salad, and is also excellent as a dressing for pasta salad.

Green Goddess Salad

This famous salad was created in 1915 at the Palace Hotel in honor of George Arliss, who was appearing in the play "The Green Goddess."

Serves 8 to 10.

2   heads of different lettuces
Shrimp, crabmeat or shredded chicken

DRESSING
8-10 anchovy fillets
1   green onion
1   clove garlic
¼   cup minced parsley
2   tablespoons fresh tarragon minced
¼   cup chopped chives
3   cups mayonnaise
¼   cup tarragon wine vinegar

Wash lettuces, dry and tear into bite-size pieces and toss together. Place on individual plates. For dressing mix together in a food processor anchovies, green onion and garlic until finely minced. Add parsley, tarragon and chives and process few seconds. Stir in mayonnaise and vinegar. Pour over greens. Garnish with shellfish or shredded chicken.

You can substitute 1½ cups low-fat buttermilk and 1½ cups low-fat sour cream for mayonnaise.

Crunchy Pea Salad

Excellent for a picnic or other event when you are asked to bring something.

Serves 6.

⅓   **cup sour cream**
2   **tablespoons red wine vinegar**
1   **tablespoon milk**
1   **teaspoon sugar**
½   **teaspoon salt**
⅛   **teaspoon garlic powder**
1   **10-ounce package frozen peas, thawed**
¾   **cup sliced water chestnuts**
3   **tablespoons sliced green onions**
2   **tablespoons cooked bacon pieces**
¼   **cup Spanish peanuts**

For dressing combine sour cream, vinegar, milk, sugar, salt and garlic powder in a small bowl. In a large bowl combine peas, water chestnuts, green onion, bacon pieces and peanuts. Add dressing to vegetables and toss lightly to coat. Cover and chill.

Thai Noodle Salad
with Spicy Peanut Sauce

Serves 8 to 10.

1½   pounds linguine noodles
1   red bell pepper, julienned
½   pound snow peas, julienned
2   medium carrots, julienned

DRESSING

¾   cup vegetable oil
¼   cup soy sauce
¼   cup rice wine vinegar
¼   cup lime juice
1   tablespoon grated fresh ginger
1   tablespoon chopped garlic
2   tablespoons chopped cilantro
1   teaspoon Asian hot sauce
1   tablespoon fish sauce
2   tablespoons brown sugar

THAI PEANUT SAUCE

1   13-ounce can coconut milk
1   tablespoon red curry paste
½   cup peanut butter
2   tablespoons lemon or lime juice
¼   cup cilantro
2   cloves garlic
1   small piece fresh ginger
1   teaspoon fish sauce
Chopped peanuts

Cook linguine according to package directions. Mix all ingredients for dressing. Toss linguine with dressing. Chill. Toss in red pepper,

Thai Noodle Salad (continued)

snow peas and carrots. Combine all ingredients for peanut sauce in blender until smooth. To serve arrange noodle salad on plate, sprinkle with peanuts and pass peanut sauce.

For variety salad may be served with grilled prawns or teriyaki chicken placed on top of salad. Marinate prawns in some of the dressing before grilling.

Apricot Couscous Salad

Serves 4 to 6.

1	cup fresh orange juice
2	tablespoons champagne vinegar or rice vinegar
¼	cup olive oil
½	cup water
2	tablespoons grated fresh ginger
1	tablespoon golden raisins
2	tablespoons currants
8-12	thinly sliced dried apricots
¼	cup finely diced red onion
2	tablespoons white wine vinegar
1	cup instant couscous
2	tablespoons toasted pine nuts

In a medium saucepan bring orange juice, champagne vinegar, olive oil and water to a boil. Turn off heat and add ginger, raisins, currants, dried apricots, onion and white wine vinegar. Put couscous in a large bowl, pour hot mixture over all and stir. Cover and let stand for 20 minutes. Add pine nuts and fluff with a fork.

Rice Salad with Arugula

Serves 8.

- 2 **cups basmati rice**
- 3 **cups chicken broth**
- 5 **tablespoons olive oil**
- ¾ **cup sliced kalamata olives**
- 3 **tablespoons fresh lemon juice**
- 1 **bunch arugula, chopped**
- ½ **cup pine nuts**
- 3 **green onions, sliced thin**
- ⅓ **cup freshly grated Parmesan cheese**
- **Salt and pepper**

Cook rice in broth, approximately 20 minutes. Fluff with fork and put in large bowl. Mix in oil and then add rest of ingredients. Serve at room temperature.

Spinach Salad with Basil and Prosciutto

Serves 6.

- 6 **cups spinach leaves**
- 2 **cups fresh basil leaves**
- ½ **cup olive oil**
- ½ **cup prosciutto ham, chopped**
- ½ **cup pine nuts**
- 2-3 **cloves garlic, pressed**
- ¾ **cup shredded Parmesan cheese**

Wash spinach and basil leaves. Discard stems and bruised leaves. Sauté prosciutto in olive oil. Just as it starts to brown, add pine nuts and continue to sauté until pine nuts start to brown. Add garlic last. Allow to cool slightly, and add to spinach and basil. Toss along with Parmesan cheese.

Curried Rice Salad

This easy recipe can be served hot or cold.

Serves 4 to 6.

⅔   **cup chicken broth**
1⅓ **cups water**
1   **cup long grain rice**
½   **cup raisins**
¼   **cup olive oil**
1   **teaspoon curry powder**
1   **tablespoon lemon juice**
1   **small green pepper, diced**
3   **green onions, thinly sliced**
1-2 **large carrots, coarsely grated**
2   **ounces sliced almonds**
Salt and pepper to taste

Bring chicken broth and water to a boil in a large saucepan. Stir in rice and return to a boil. Simmer, covered, for 20 to 25 minutes, until rice is done. Put raisins in a small pot and cover with water. Bring to a boil, remove from heat and let raisins plump.

Stir curry powder and lemon juice into oil. When rice is cooked, stir in seasoned oil. Drain raisins and add with green pepper, green onions, grated carrots, and sliced almonds. Add salt and pepper or more lemon juice, if needed. Serve room temperature or chilled.

Low-Fat California Chinese Chicken Salad

This is a very different version of the usual Chinese Chicken Salad.

Serves 6.

½	**cup rice vinegar**
3	**tablespoons soy sauce**
1½	**tablespoons minced fresh ginger**
1	**tablespoon sugar**
1	**tablespoon dry mustard mixed with 1 tablespoon water**
1	**tablespoon sesame oil**
4-5	**ounces cellophane noodles**
½	**pound Chinese pea pods, strings removed**
2½-3	**cups cooked chicken, boned and skinned**
1	**tablespoon salad oil**
2	**cloves garlic, thinly sliced**
1	**cup red onion, thinly sliced**
2	**tablespoons lemon juice**
2	**large red or yellow bell peppers, diced or sliced**
6	**cups salad greens**
½	**cup fresh cilantro, finely chopped**
	Cilantro leaves

For dressing, mix together rice vinegar, soy sauce, ginger, sugar, mustard mixture and sesame oil.

Bring 2 quarts water to boil. Add noodles, return to boiling and stir once to keep noodles from sticking together. Remove from heat and let stand until barely tender to bite, 10 to 15 minutes. (If they are cooked too long, they will stick together.) Pour into a colander and rinse with cold water. If desired, with scissors, snip noodles into shorter pieces. Drain 10 minutes, then mix with about ⅓ of dressing. Boil peas until bright green, about 1 minute. Drain and immerse in ice water.

Low-Fat California Chinese Chicken Salad (continued)

Tear chicken into thin strips and put in large bowl. Pour 1 tablespoon oil into a wok. Add garlic and stir-fry until pale gold, about 1 minute. Add onion, lemon juice, and 2 tablespoons water and stir-fry until liquid evaporates and onion is very limp. Add to chicken.

Mix salad greens with cilantro. Arrange on plate. Mound noodles in center of greens. Arrange chicken mixture, peas and peppers decoratively around noodles. Top with remaining dressing and garnish with cilantro, if desired.

Oriental Turkey and Fruit Salad

Serves 4.

2	**cups cooked white turkey meat, cubed**
¼	**cup soy sauce**
4	**cups diagonally sliced celery**
4	**pitted purple plums, diced**
4	**small yellow unpeeled apples, diced**
¼	**cup raisins**
¼	**cup low-fat mayonnaise**
¼	**cup low-fat yogurt**
	Curry powder to taste
	Tabasco sauce, optional
	Crisp lettuce leaves
¼	**cup dry-roasted peanuts**

Sprinkle turkey with soy sauce and stir well. Add celery, plums, apples and raisins. Stir in mayonnaise, yogurt, curry powder and Tabasco sauce. To serve, pile on lettuce leaves or mound in individual salad bowls. Sprinkle with nuts. Pass additional soy sauce and Tabasco, if desired.

Tomato Bread Salad with Grilled Chicken

Serves 8.

2	**pounds chicken thighs, boned and skinned**
8	**ounces good quality croutons**
3	**large ripe tomatoes, seeded and diced**
1	**cup frozen corn, thawed**
½	**cup pitted kalamata olives, halved**
¼	**cup chopped red onions**
4	**green onions, sliced thin**
3	**tablespoons capers, drained**
½	**bunch fresh basil, chopped**
2	**cloves garlic**
3	**tablespoons balsamic vinegar**
½	**cup olive oil**

Salt and pepper to taste

Grill chicken thighs until done. Slice on the diagonal and set aside. Combine the croutons, tomatoes, corn, olives, red onions, green onions, capers and basil. In a blender combine garlic, vinegar and olive oil. Mix with the chicken and salad ingredients. Toss well and add salt and pepper. Serve immediately.

Crab Louis

This is a favorite salad in the Bay Area.

Serves 4.

1	**cup mayonnaise**
¼	**cup whipping cream**
¼	**cup chili sauce**
¼	**cup chopped green pepper**
¼	**cup chopped green onion**

Salt

Lemon juice

2	**heads iceberg lettuce**
1½-2	**pounds fresh Dungeness crabmeat (about 2 crabs)**
4	**large tomatoes**
4	**hard-boiled eggs**

Mix together mayonnaise, whipping cream, chili sauce, green pepper and green onions. Season with salt and lemon juice to taste. Arrange outer leaves of lettuce on 4 large plates. Shred the remaining lettuce and arrange in the center of the large leaves. Place crabmeat on top of shredded lettuce, reserving large pieces of crab legs. Cut tomatoes and eggs into sixths. Arrange around crab. Pour Louis dressing over crab and garnish with reserved crab legs.

For additional garnishes include olives, asparagus, sliced cucumbers, artichoke hearts, and avocado slices.

Molded Salmon Salad

Serve with Avocado or Dill Sauce

Serves 4 to 6.

1	envelope unflavored gelatin
¼	cup cold water
¾	cup boiling water
2	tablespoons sugar
1	tablespoon lemon juice
1	tablespoon vinegar
2	teaspoons grated onion
½	teaspoon salt
½	teaspoon horseradish
1	pound fresh salmon, poached and flaked
½	cup mayonnaise
¼	cup finely diced celery

Soften the gelatin in cold water. Add boiling water and stir until gelatin is dissolved. Add sugar, lemon juice, vinegar, onion, salt, and horseradish. Chill the mixture until it begins to set. Stir in the salmon from which any skin or bones has been removed. Add mayonnaise and celery. Grease a 3-cup mold lightly with mayonnaise, and spoon mixture into it. Chill 5 hours or overnight. Unmold and serve with either sauce.

AVOCADO SAUCE

Makes about 1¼ cups.

1	large ripe avocado
½	cup sour cream
½	teaspoon salt

Seed, peel and mash avocado. Mix in sour cream and salt and chill thoroughly.

Molded Salmon Salad (continued)

DILL SAUCE

Makes about 2½ cups.

- 1½ **cups dairy sour cream**
- 1 **cup mayonnaise**
- 2 **tablespoons lemon juice**
- 2 **tablespoons fresh dill weed**

Combine all ingredients and chill.

Thai Shrimp Salad

Serves 4.

- 2 **cups water**
- 1 **pound shrimp or prawns, shelled and deveined**
- 2 **stalks lemon grass, thinly sliced**
- 4 **kaffir lime leaves, thinly diced**
- ½ **cup mint leaves**
- 2 **tablespoons chopped green onion**
- 1 **tablespoon chopped cilantro**
- 1 **teaspoon ground Thai chili pepper**
- ¼ **cup fish sauce**
- ¼ **cup lime juice**
- **Lettuce leaves**
- 1 **cucumber, thinly sliced**

Heat the water to boiling in a large saucepan and add the shrimp. Blanch for 2 to 3 minutes or until pink and remove. Place in a bowl. Add the lemon grass, lime leaves, mint, green onion and cilantro leaves. Mix well. Sprinkle ground chili pepper over the mixture, and pour on fish sauce and lime juice. Gently toss to combine. Place on top of lettuce leaves. Garnish with cucumber.

Curried Seafood Salad

Serves 6 to 8.

½ **pound fresh crabmeat**
½ **pound fresh bay shrimp**
1 **10-ounce package frozen peas, thawed**
1 **cup diced celery**
2 **green onions, thinly sliced**
¾ **cup mayonnaise**
1 **tablespoon lemon juice**
1 **tablespoon soy sauce**
⅛ **teaspoon garlic salt**
½-1 **teaspoon curry powder**
1 **5-ounce can chow mein noodles**
Lettuce

Mix together crab, shrimp, peas, celery and green onions and chill. For dressing combine mayonnaise, lemon juice, soy sauce, garlic salt and curry powder. Just before serving combine crab-shrimp mixture with dressing. Add noodles. Serve on a bed of your favorite lettuce.

Green Salad with Seared Tuna

Serves 4.

¾	pound mixed greens
1	medium daikon radish, julienned
1	red bell pepper, julienned
6	radishes, thinly sliced
¼	pound green beans, blanched
4	tuna fillets

Salt and pepper to taste

1	tablespoon vegetable oil

ORIENTAL DRESSING

Zest and juice of 1 lime

Zest and juice of 1 orange

1	tablespoon rice wine vinegar
2	cloves garlic, minced
1	tablespoon chopped ginger
2	tablespoons Asian chili sauce
1	teaspoon wasabi powder
2	tablespoons hot water
¾	cup vegetable oil

Soy sauce to taste

Place all vegetables in salad bowl. Season tuna fillets with salt and pepper. Heat oil in cast iron skillet until smoking hot. Sear 1 to 2 minutes on each side for rare, 2 to 3 minutes for medium. Slice thinly. Mix together all dressing ingredients. Pour ⅓ cup dressing over vegetables in a bowl and toss. Divide among 4 plates and top with thin-sliced tuna. Serve immediately. Pass remaining dressing at the table.

Mediterranean Salad

Serves 4.

1	medium head butter lettuce
½	cup oil
¼	cup vinegar
2	tablespoons Dijon mustard
¼	teaspoon dried tarragon
¼	teaspoon dried dill
1	clove garlic, crushed
4	new potatoes
2	green onions, finely sliced
½	pound whole green beans, cooked
1	7½-ounce can tuna
2	tablespoons capers
2	large tomatoes, cut in 8 wedges
4	hard cooked eggs, cut in half
12	pitted black olives
4	anchovies, cut in half lengthwise

Wash lettuce and refrigerate. Combine oil, vinegar, mustard, tarragon, dill and garlic. Cook potatoes in boiling water, then slice about ⅜ inch thick. Pour ¼ of dressing over potatoes while warm. Add ½ of green onions. Stir, cover and let marinate for a few hours. Pour ¼ dressing over beans, along with the rest of the green onions. Let marinate. Line plates with large lettuce leaves. Tear remaining lettuce into bite-size pieces and mound in center of plates. Drain tuna and flake. Place in center of lettuce. Sprinkle with capers. Arrange potatoes, beans, tomatoes, eggs and olives around tuna. Place ½ an anchovy on each ½ egg. Pour remaining dressing over all and serve.

North Beach Italian Dressing

Makes about ¾ cup.

- ¾ **cup oil (part olive oil, if desired)**
- 2 **tablespoons minced onion**
- 1 **tablespoon Parmesan cheese**
- 2 **teaspoons salt**
- ¾ **teaspoon dry mustard**
- ¾ **teaspoon dry basil**
- ¾ **teaspoon dry oregano**
- ¾ **teaspoon sugar**
- ¾ **teaspoon pepper**
- ¾ **teaspoon Worcestershire sauce**
- ¼ **cup red wine vinegar**
- 1 **tablespoon lemon juice**
- 1 **tablespoon capers**

Mix all ingredients except vinegar and lemon juice and capers in a blender for about 30 seconds. Add remaining ingredients and blend again. Recipe may be doubled.

Poppyseed Dressing

This is terrific with fruit and nut salads or spinach salad.

Makes about 2½ cups.

- ¾ **cup sugar**
- 1 **teaspoon dry mustard**
- **Pinch salt**
- ⅓ **cup raspberry vinegar**
- 1 **cup salad oil**
- ⅓ **cup poppy seeds**

Combine sugar, mustard, salt and vinegar in blender. Add oil gradually at low speed. Stir in poppy seeds.

Roasted Garlic Dressing

Try this over mixed greens.
It can also be used as a marinade for poultry or meat.

Makes about 1½ cups.

1   head garlic, cut in half horizontally
2   cloves garlic, minced
⅓   cup olive oil
¼   cup red wine vinegar
1   tablespoon Dijon mustard
1   teaspoon chopped chives
1   teaspoon chopped basil
Salt and pepper

Spray cut halves of garlic with cooking spray and place cut side down on sprayed baking pan. Bake at 325 degrees for 30 minutes or until sharp knife is easily inserted in a clove. Cool and squeeze insides of roasted garlic cloves into bowl and mash. Add minced garlic, olive oil, red wine vinegar, mustard, chives, basil, salt and pepper. Stir until well blended.

Vegetables and Side Dishes

The Golden Gate National Recreation Area

Climb above the bustle of Bridgeway, above the bright mosaic of Sausalito's hillside homes, above Highway 101, and you arrive at the gateway to a wilderness landscape stretching far as the eye can see - south to the Golden Gate, west to the Pacific, and north to Mt. Tamalpais. Here, just minutes from downtown Sausalito and the heart of San Francisco, is the Golden Gate National Recreation Area (GGNRA) - home to lupine, poppies, bobcats and the Mission Blue Butterfly.

A boon for Sausalitans, the GGNRA has been a much appreciated, much utilized parkland for all Bay Area residents since it was established by act of Congress in 1972. At that time some 25,000 acres, spanning the San Francisco shoreline and extending up the Marin Coast to Point Reyes, was set aside for public use, connecting already existing parks. In 1983 the park was officially dedicated to the memory of San Francisco Congressman Phillip Burton, who had fought so hard for its creation. Largely through the incorporation of additional public lands, the GGNRA has tripled its original size.

Just over Wolfback Ridge, beside the Pacific shore, the Headlands Visitor Center provides information on the many uses of this great open space preserve. For Sausalito strollers, hikers, equestrians, bikers, and bird-watchers, our piece of the GGNRA remains an ever accessible daily miracle, just footsteps from our back doors.

By Jaqueline Kudler

Artichokes Romani

These artichokes are rich and meaty, and delicious as a side dish or as a first course with crusty bread to soak up the juices. Serve them halved or quartered.

Serves 4.

4	**large artichokes**
2-3	**lemons, cut in half**
	Coarse salt
⅓	**cup minced fresh mint leaves**
1	**tablespoon minced garlic**
½	**cup olive oil, divided**

Trim off all tough green outer leaves and pare away at the stem, removing woody part and keeping stem as long as possible, until the pale green tender part is exposed. Using cut lemon rub all cut surfaces. With a stainless steel knife cut off about 1- to 2-inches from the top, then cut in half or in quarters. With a small spoon dig out all of the fuzzy choke and pull off any interior leaves that have prickly tips. Immerse in water that has juice of ½ lemon in it.

Drain and lightly salt the interiors. Combine mint, garlic, 2 table-spoons olive oil and salt to taste. Put mixture in center of each artichoke. Arrange artichokes cut side up in a pan just large enough to contain them. Drizzle with remaining olive oil. Add water to come ½ of the way up. Salt lightly and add remaining lemons, cut up, to water. Bring to a boil, then simmer, covered, until tender but firm. The time will vary depending on cut size. Remove with a slotted spoon. Bring remaining liquid to a boil and reduce until it is a nice syrupy liquid. Pour over artichokes. Serve at room temperature.

Can be made up to 2 days ahead.

Danish Red Cabbage

Serves 6.

1	**medium red cabbage**
4	**tablespoons butter**
1	**tablespoon honey**
1	**teaspoon salt**
⅓	**cup water**
2	**tablespoons cider vinegar**
¼	**cup currant jelly**
1	**apple, cored and grated**

Wash cabbage, remove core and outer leaves, and shred or chop fine. There will be about 8 cups. Combine butter, honey, salt, water and vinegar in an ovenproof 4 or 5-quart casserole. Bring mixture to a boil and add cabbage. Mix thoroughly. Bring to a boil again, cover tightly and bake at 350 degrees for 2 hours. Check occasionally so that it does not dry out. Add more liquid if necessary. About 10 minutes before it is done, add currant jelly and apple. Cover and finish cooking. It is best made day before and reheated.

Bourbon Glazed Carrots

Serves 8.

8	**large carrots, or 3 pounds baby carrots**
2	**tablespoons butter**
¼	**cup maple syrup**
¼	**cup bourbon**
1	**teaspoon tarragon**

Scrape carrots and cut into julienne strips. Cook carrots for 6 minutes or until tender, but firm. Drain. Combine butter, maple syrup, bourbon and tarragon. Cook down until slightly thick and syrupy. Pour over hot carrots.

Wilted Red Chard
with Balsamic Dressing

Serve this as a vegetable side dish or
add a few ingredients and serve as a luncheon salad.

Serves 4.

2	**tablespoons olive oil**
½	**onion, chopped**
2	**cloves garlic, crushed**
1	**bunch of chard, washed and dried**
2	**tablespoons fresh thyme leaves**
	Salt and pepper to taste
1-2	**tablespoons balsamic vinegar**

Heat olive oil in a pan with a tight fitting lid. Add onion and sauté on high heat, stirring occasionally until just golden. Add garlic to pan and stir to mix. Cut chard stems into ½-inch dice. Cut chard leaves into strips. Add chard stems and stir until stems are crisp, but tender. Add chard leaves to pan with thyme, salt and pepper. Turn up heat, toss together and pour balsamic vinegar into pan. Put on lid, take pan off heat and shake well. Let steam 1 to 2 minutes. Serve while warm. For a sweeter taste use mango or raspberry vinegar.

To make this into a luncheon salad, add 1 green apple, cored and sliced, and ¼ cup of walnut halves when you add the garlic. When ready to serve, toss in ¼ cup crumbled blue cheese.

Two-in-One Corn Pudding

This is basically a corn pudding recipe expanded to a corn custard and bread pudding. A wonderful dinner party side dish as a custard alone, or a Corn Bread Pudding for a buffet table. This can be a hearty dish for a vegetarian as well.

Serves 10.

CORN CUSTARD PUDDING

2	eggs beaten
3	tablespoons flour
2	tablespoons sugar
½	teaspoon salt
¼	teaspoon paprika
2	cups milk or half-and-half
2½	cups creamed corn (a 15-ounce can contains 1¾ cups of corn)
1	tablespoon butter

Combine all ingredients and pour into a 10-inch glass pie pan. Bake in a 350 degree oven for one hour or until the custard sets. Serves 6 to 8.

CORN BREAD PUDDING

1	loaf sliced white bread, trim crusts and let sit out a few hours to dry.
2	tablespoons soft butter-spread on the top layer of bread
1	cup Asiago or good quality Parmesan or Romano cheese

Prepare a double recipe of the Corn Custard Pudding up to the point of adding the corn. Reserve 2 cups of the custard to pour as a top layer on the casserole. Add the corn to the remaining custard and mix well.

Cover the bottom of a greased 3-quart rectangular casserole with a layer of the trimmed bread, placing the bread close together. Pour the corn pudding on top of the bread. Sprinkle half of the cheese on

Two-in-One Corn Pudding (continued)

top of the corn mixture. Repeat with second layer of buttered bread slices. Pour the reserved 2 cups of custard over the top layer of the buttered bread. Sprinkle with the remaining cheese.

Bake in a 350 degree oven for one and a half hours until golden and the custard is set. It will puff up and then settle down after being removed from the oven. Serve promptly. Cut into squares and serve with a spatula or serve with a serving spoon.

Corn Pudding

Serves 4 to 6.

3	**tablespoons butter**
3	**tablespoons flour**
1	**tablespoon sugar**
½	**cup light cream**
¾	**cup milk**
1	**15-ounce can whole kernel corn, drained**
1	**15-ounce can cream-style corn**
3	**whole eggs**

Melt butter and stir in flour. Add sugar, light cream and milk. Heat over medium heat until thickened, stirring constantly. Stir in whole kernel corn and cream-style corn. Remove from heat and whisk in 3 eggs, one at a time. Pour into a 2-quart casserole. Place in a pan with 2 inches of water and bake uncovered at 350 degrees for 1½ hours. When done, the center should be firm when shaken. Cut into squares to serve.

Spinach Squares

Serves 6.

2	**10-ounce packages frozen chopped spinach**
3	**tablespoons butter**
1	**small onion, chopped**
¼	**pound mushrooms, sliced**
4	**eggs**
¼	**cup dry bread crumbs**
¼	**cup grated Parmesan cheese, divided**
1	**can cream of mushroom soup**
¼	**teaspoon pepper**
¼	**teaspoon dry basil**
¼	**teaspoon dry oregano**

Thaw spinach and squeeze dry. Melt butter and sauté onions and mushrooms. Beat eggs and add bread crumbs, 2 tablespoons cheese, mushroom soup, pepper, basil and oregano. Add spinach and mushroom mixture. Turn into 9-inch square pan. Cover with remaining cheese. Bake at 325 degrees for 35 to 50 minutes until firm. Serve warm.

Christ Church, at the intersection of San Carlos and Santa Rosa Avenues, was built without nails by shipbuilders in 1882. It is the oldest surviving church structure in Sausalito.

Baked Ratatouille

Serves 8.

⅓	**cup olive oil**
2	**small onions, chopped**
2	**small eggplants, peeled and chopped**
2	**cloves garlic, minced**
1	**teaspoon salt**
½	**teaspoon white pepper**
2	**teaspoons dry thyme**
½	**teaspoon dry basil**
¼	**teaspoon dry oregano**
3	**ripe tomatoes, sliced**
3	**zucchini, sliced**

Heat oil in large pan, and add onions and eggplant. Toss thoroughly in oil and cook 10 minutes. Add all other ingredients except tomatoes and zucchini. Cover and simmer 45 minutes. Remove cover and cook an additional 30 minutes until excess moisture has evaporated. Adjust seasonings. It should be like a vegetable puree. Place puree in greased baking dish and arrange tomatoes and zucchini in rows on top of puree. Sprinkle with more salt, pepper and thyme, and drizzle with olive oil. Bake at 375 degrees for 20 minutes.

Caponata

This is a tasty version of ratatouille. Great for picnics and as an accompaniment to grilled meat, especially lamb. If you cut the vegetables in smaller pieces, you can use it as an hors d'oeuvre spread on crackers or a sliced baguette.

Serves 10 to 12.

½	cup olive oil
1	eggplant, peeled and cut into ¾-inch cubes
2	bell peppers (red, green or yellow), cut into ¾-inch cubes
2	large onions, diced
2-4	cloves garlic, minced
1	28-ounce can tomatoes, chopped
⅓	cup wine vinegar
1	tablespoon sugar
2-4	tablespoons capers
2	tablespoons tomato paste
½	bunch parsley, chopped
½	cup green olives, coarsely chopped
½	teaspoon ground pepper

Salt to taste

2	tablespoons fresh or 2 teaspoons dried basil, or oregano
½	cup pine nuts, toasted

In olive oil sauté eggplant, peppers, onions, garlic and tomatoes in a large heavy saucepan for 20 minutes or until tender. Add vinegar, sugar, capers, tomato paste, parsley, olives, pepper, salt and herbs. Cover and simmer for 15 minutes. Let cool, and add pine nuts.

This lasts 3 weeks in the refrigerator, and tastes best when at room temperature.

Green Vegetables
with Hazelnut Dressing

This is a pretty dish for a buffet and great for a picnic.
The hazelnuts add an interesting crunch.

Serves 10 to 14.

1	**pound asparagus**
1	**pound green beans**
1	**bunch broccoli, cut into florets**
1	**pound snap peas or snow peas, strings removed**

HAZELNUT DRESSING

1¼	**cups olive oil**
¼	**cup red wine vinegar or rice vinegar**
⅓	**cup orange juice**
2	**tablespoons grated orange peel**
¾	**cup hazelnuts, toasted and finely chopped**

Cut asparagus into about 2-inch lengths. Blanch all vegetables in boiling water until bright green. Drain and rinse quickly in cold water. Chill in a large bowl.

Whisk dressing ingredients together. Just before serving or no more than 2 hours ahead, add hazelnuts to the dressing and pour over the vegetables.

Other combinations of vegetables can be used.

Wild Mushroom Pudding

*This is a standard strata or bread pudding recipe. The mushrooms
may be replaced with any of the following: corn, diced green
peppers, pimientos, peas, chopped ham or bacon.*

Serves 8.

1½	**pounds mixed mushrooms (porcini, cremini, shiitake, domestic, etc.), sliced**
3	**green onions, chopped**
12	**tablespoons butter, divided**
16	**slices good bread, crusts removed and cut into 1-inch pieces**
1	**pound Swiss or Gruyère cheese, grated**
8	**eggs**
2	**cups milk**
1	**teaspoon salt**
½	**teaspoon pepper**
2	**teaspoons dry mustard**

Sauté mushrooms and green onions in 6 tablespoons butter for 15
minutes. Grease a 2-quart casserole. Put ⅓ of bread in bottom of
dish. Cover with ½ of mushrooms and ½ of cheese. Add ⅓ more
bread, the rest of the mushroom and cheese, and the last ⅓ of bread.
Mix together eggs, milk, salt, pepper and dry mustard. Pour over
other ingredients. Pour 6 tablespoons melted butter over top. Cover
and refrigerate overnight. Bake at 375 degrees, covered, in a pan of
water for 1 hour and 15 minutes. Cut into squares to serve.

Festive Onions

Recipe can be made ahead and easily doubled.

Serves 6 to 8.

1	**pound small white onions**
1	**cup water**
1	**tablespoon brown sugar**
1	**teaspoon salt**
¼	**teaspoon paprika**

Pepper to taste

2	**tablespoons chopped or slivered almonds**
4	**tablespoons butter**
2	**tablespoons flour**
1	**teaspoon Worcestershire sauce**

To peel onions easily, prick with dinner fork and cover with boiling water. Let set for 10 minutes. Drain and peel. Combine water, brown sugar, salt, paprika and pepper in saucepan and bring to a boil. Add onions, cover, and simmer for 30 minutes. Drain. Save liquid. Place onions in greased 1-quart casserole. Slightly brown almonds in butter and flour. Stir in liquid from onions. Stir and cook until thickened. Add Worcestershire. Pour sauce over onions. (It can now be covered and frozen, or refrigerated until dinner.) Bake at 375 degrees for 25 minutes. If frozen, bake at 350 degrees for 30 to 40 minutes. Excellent with turkey or roast beef.

Onion Tart

Serves 8.

3	**or more onions, finely chopped**
½	**cup butter**
2	**teaspoons salt**
½	**teaspoon cumin**
4	**eggs, lightly beaten**
4	**or more ounces Swiss or Gruyère cheese, grated**
1	**tablespoon Dijon mustard**
¾	**cup cream**
¾	**cup plain yogurt**
1	**pre-baked 10-inch pie crust**

Sauté onions in butter for 20 minutes, until soft. Remove from heat and add salt and cumin. Whisk together eggs, cheese, mustard, cream and yogurt. Add onions. Pour into pie shell. Bake at 375 degrees for 30 minutes, or until set.

Sweet Potato and Orange Casserole

Serves 8 to 10.

2	**pounds sweet potatoes**
3	**navel oranges**
1	**tablespoon cornstarch**
1	**cup orange juice**
3	**tablespoons honey or maple syrup**
⅛	**teaspoon ground cloves**
2	**tablespoons slivered almonds**
2	**tablespoons unsweetened shredded coconut**

Place the sweet potatoes in a large saucepan, cover with water and cook until easily pierced with a fork. Drain and set aside until cool enough to handle. Peel, then cut into ¼-inch slices. Reserve.

Finely grate enough peel from the oranges to equal 2 teaspoons. Set aside. Peel oranges, removing all the white pith. Cut oranges crosswise into ¼-inch slices. Mix gently with the sweet potatoes. Transfer to a nonstick, spray-coated 9-inch x 13-inch baking dish.

In a small saucepan mix the orange peel, cornstarch , orange juice, honey and cloves. Cook over medium heat, stirring constantly, until mixture thickens. Pour over sweet potatoes and oranges. Sprinkle with almonds and coconut. Bake at 375 degrees for 15 minutes or until heated through.

Baked Yellow Squash with Red Bell Pepper

Serves 4.

1	medium onion, chopped
3-4	cloves garlic, minced or crushed
3-4	yellow crookneck squash, sliced ¼-inch thick
¼	cup fresh basil, including stems, chopped fine
1	red bell pepper, diced
2-3	tablespoons olive oil

Salt and pepper to taste

1	tablespoon butter, optional

Combine all vegetables with olive oil and seasonings in an oven-proof dish. Dot with butter. Bake tightly covered at 350 degrees for 30 to 40 minutes.

Zucchini Frittata

Serves 8 to 10.

6	**zucchini**
3	**eggs**
3	**green onions and tops, chopped**
¾	**cup bread crumbs**
¾	**cup flour**
¼	**cup chopped parsley**
¼	**teaspoon fines herbes**
¼	**teaspoon oregano**
½	**cup shredded Monterey Jack cheese**

Salt and pepper to taste

2	**tablespoons butter**
¼	**cup Parmesan cheese**

Grate or chop zucchini coarsely. Mix together all ingredients except butter. Pour into 9-inch x 12-inch greased pan. Dot top with butter. Sprinkle with Parmesan cheese. Bake at 350 degrees for 45 to 50 minutes. Cut into squares to serve.

In 1885 there were 1,500 residents and eight hotels in Sausalito.

Roasted Garlic Custard

*If you dare to serve this as a smashing alternative to potatoes, rice,
or grains, you will be asked for the recipe for years to come*

Serves 8 to 10.

3-4 heads of garlic

Olive oil

6   eggs

3   egg whites

2   cups heavy cream

Salt

White pepper

Preheat oven to 375 degrees. Cut the tops off heads of garlic. Place heads on a large square of aluminum foil and drizzle with olive oil. Wrap tightly and bake 1 to 1½ hours until garlic is very soft. Let cool. Squeeze the garlic gently from the skins and mash.

Set oven to 250 degrees and put a kettle of water to boil. Butter metal muffin tin or individual molds. Beat eggs with whites until well blended. Add cream and mix well. Add roasted garlic. Mix and pass through fine sieve. Pour into buttered molds until ¾ full. Place muffin tin or molds in pan of boiling water which comes ½ way up the sides. Bake until firm about 1 hour and 15 minutes for a muffin tin, longer if ceramic mold is used. The custard is set when a knife inserted in the center comes out clean. Serve immediately or set aside for a couple of hours. To reheat, place baked custard back in the hot water bath for 7 to 10 minutes before serving. Invert onto plates to serve.

Potato Cheese Casserole

Serves 4 to 6.

2	**pounds russet potatoes**
1½	**cups sour cream**
1½	**cups shredded Gruyère cheese**
1	**medium carrot, peeled and shredded**
¼	**cup minced onion**
2	**tablespoons minced parsley**
1	**teaspoon salt**
½	**teaspoon dried dill weed, optional**
⅛	**teaspoon pepper**
	Paprika

Boil potatoes in their jackets until tender. Peel and shred. Combine potatoes with sour cream, 1 cup of the cheese, carrot, onion, parsley, salt, dill and pepper. Turn into a buttered 1½-quart casserole. Sprinkle with remaining ½ cup cheese and paprika. Bake at 350 degrees for 30 to 40 minutes.

Armenian Rice Pilaf

Serves 4 generously.

4	**tablespoons butter or margarine**
½	**cup vermicelli or coil fideo (very thin curly pasta)**
1	**cup long grain rice**
2½	**cups chicken broth**
	Salt to taste

Melt butter in 1½ to 2-quart saucepan. Break up the pasta into small pieces. Fry in butter until golden brown. Add the rice and sauté for a minute or so until the rice is coated with butter. Add the chicken broth and salt. Bring to a boil, then lower to barely a simmer and cook for 20 to 25 minutes until all of the broth is absorbed. Do not stir while cooking. Stir just before serving.

Bulgur may be substituted for the rice to make Bulgur Pilaf.

Masala Bhat (Curried Rice)

Serves 6.

1	cup Basmati rice
3	tablespoons oil
1	teaspoon black mustard seeds
1	teaspoon cumin seeds
2	bay leaves
2	whole red chiles
1	teaspoon turmeric
½	cup sliced onions
1½	cups water
¼	cup slivered almonds
1	carrot, julienned
1	teaspoon cumin powder
1	teaspoon ground coriander
1	cup peas

Salt to taste

Juice of ½ lemon

Cilantro

Soak rice in cold water. Drain. Heat oil in skillet and add mustard seeds, cumin seeds, bay leaves and red chiles. When mustard seeds pop, add turmeric, sliced onions and rice, stirring until golden. Add water, almonds, carrot, cumin powder and coriander. Cover and simmer on low heat for approximately 20 minutes. Rice should be slightly al dente. Fluff and add peas, lemon juice and salt. Garnish with cilantro.

Fennel Risotto

Serves 4.

5	**cups low-fat, low-salt chicken broth**
3	**tablespoons olive oil**
½	**cup finely minced onion**
1	**clove garlic, minced**
1	**small bulb fresh fennel, top removed, bulb chopped fine**
1½	**cups Arborio rice**
½	**cup dry white wine**
½	**cup grated Parmesan cheese**
1	**tablespoon finely minced green fennel leaves**

Bring broth to a low simmer in a saucepan. In a heavy large skillet, heat olive oil and add onion, garlic and chopped fennel, and sauté until onion softens. Add the rice to the skillet and stir to coat the rice. Add wine and stir until completely absorbed. Using a ladle, add hot broth ½ cup at a time, stirring frequently to prevent sticking. Continue adding broth, but wait until each addition is absorbed before adding next ½ cup. After about 18 minutes, when the rice is tender, but firm, add the rest of broth and again cook until broth is absorbed. Turn off heat. Add Parmesan cheese and stir. Serve immediately and garnish with minced fennel leaves.

If you do not serve immediately, reserve ¾ cup of the broth and incorporate it just before serving.

Fried Rice

This dish provides an easy way to use leftovers to create a delicious side dish or, with the addition of ham or shrimp, turns into a quick one-dish meal. Always be sure that the cooked rice is dry and cold before using.

Serves 4.

4	cups cooked rice
3	tablespoons salad oil
1	cup sautéed sliced mushrooms
2	green onions, thinly sliced
1	teaspoon chopped fresh ginger
2-3	eggs, scrambled
1-2	tablespoons soy sauce
1	tablespoon rice wine or dry sherry
½	cup slivered almonds

In a wok or frying pan cook rice in oil for about 5 minutes, or until lightly browned, stirring constantly. Add mushrooms, green onions and ginger, and cook for 3 minutes.

Add scrambled eggs. Season with soy sauce and rice wine. Add nuts and stir.

For variety add ½ cup of peas or broccoli florets cut in small pieces. For a main dish add ½ cup of cooked shrimp, diced ham, pork or chicken.

Lemon Pilaf
with Currants and Almonds

Serves 4 to 6.

2	**tablespoons butter or oil, divided**
1	**tablespoon minced onion**
1	**cup white rice**
1½	**cups seasoned chicken stock**
¼	**cup lemon juice**
	Zest of 1 lemon, finely minced
2	**tablespoons currants**
¼	**cup slivered almonds, toasted**

In a 2-quart saucepan, heat 1 tablespoon butter and sauté onion until soft. Add rice, and stir until the grains of rice are coated with butter. Stir in chicken stock, lemon juice, zest and currants. Bring to a boil and then lower heat and cover. Simmer for about 20 minutes, or until all liquid is absorbed. Stir in remaining tablespoon of butter and almonds.

Wild Rice Casserole

Serves 10 to 12.

1	**pound mushrooms**
4	**tablespoons butter**
1	**cup wild rice**
1	**cup canned tomatoes, diced**
½	**cup chopped onion**
1½	**cups boiling water**
2	**2¼-ounce cans chopped ripe olives**
1	**teaspoon salt**
½	**teaspoon pepper**
1	**cup cubed cheddar cheese, optional**

Wash, slice and sauté mushrooms in butter. Wash wild rice well by letting cold water run through. Mix all ingredients and spoon into a greased casserole dish. Stir to mix well. Cover and bake at 325 degrees for 2 hours.

Main Dishes and Pasta

The Herring Season

"It's the herring season again!" Each December the shout echoes across the water and over the hills as Richardson's Bay comes alive with the largest commercial fishery south of British Columbia. Although the Pacific Herring swim into the Bay in October, it is not until a month or so later that the reproduction process is complete and the harvest can begin. The colorful scene that results is unequaled.

The drama is set against a backdrop of winter clouds and intermittent fog, rain and sunshine. The rumble of boats and shouts of fishermen, the screech of gulls and barking of sea lions create a soundtrack that travels up the canyons and hills of the town. The take is usually bountiful and highly profitable, with many tons brought in each year. Quotas are controlled by the California Department of Fish and Game, based on an estimate of the season's population. Fishing permits are highly coveted. The roe from this annual herring harvest is predominantly sold in Japan where salted roe, or "kazunoko," is in high demand.

Local residents also partake of the bounty, gathering roe-encrusted seaweed along the shoreline or fishing from piers. Once harvested, the Pacific Herring is delicious pickled, baked or grilled.

By Shelby Van Meter

Crustless Spinach Quiche

Serves 6 to 8.

2	tablespoons vegetable oil
1	large onion, chopped
½	red bell pepper, chopped
½	green bell pepper, chopped
½	pound ham, cut in ¼-inch cubes
1	10-ounce package frozen spinach, thawed, drained
6	eggs
½	pound Jack cheese with jalapeño peppers, grated

Salt and pepper to taste
Few drops Tabasco sauce

Preheat oven to 350 degrees. Butter and dust with flour a 10-inch pie pan. Heat oil in skillet over medium-high heat. Add onion and peppers and sauté until wilted. Add ham and spinach and cook until excess moisture is evaporated. Let cool. Beat eggs. Add grated cheese. Stir into onion-spinach mixture and season to taste with salt and pepper. If you wish, add a few drops Tabasco sauce. Turn into pie plate. Bake until a toothpick comes out clean, 30 to 45 minutes.

By 1892 Sausalito was established as a beautiful resort town and suburb of San Francisco. In the early 1900's it was known as a "wide open" town. By the 1920's it was a hotbed of bootlegging.

Egg and Sausage Strata

A great do-ahead brunch recipe.

Serves 6.

8	slices firm bread, crusts removed
2	cups grated cheddar cheese
2	cups grated Jack cheese
1	pound sausages, cooked and cut up
1	4-ounce can diced green chiles
8	eggs (if desired use only 4 yolks)
2	cups milk
1	teaspoon oregano
¼	teaspoon garlic powder
¼	teaspoon prepared mustard
1	teaspoon salt
½	teaspoon pepper

Cut bread into small to medium squares. Sprinkle bread on bottom of greased 9-inch x 13-inch casserole. Sprinkle with cheddar cheese, sausage, Jack cheese and green chiles. Mix together eggs, milk, oregano, garlic powder, prepared mustard, salt and pepper. Pour over cheese mixture. Refrigerate overnight. Bake at 325 degrees for 1 hour uncovered. Let stand 10 minutes before serving.

Savory Cheesecake

The rich flavors of this dish go well with any full-bodied red wine.

Serves 8 or more.

¾	cup toasted bread crumbs
¾	cup toasted walnuts, finely chopped
3	tablespoons unsalted butter, melted
¾	pound aged Asiago cheese, grated
1¼	pounds cream cheese, at room temperature
4	eggs
1	medium clove garlic, minced
1	tablespoon fresh tarragon, minced

Salt and pepper

Preheat oven to 350 degrees. Place bread crumbs, walnuts and butter in food processor and blend well. Press into bottom of 8-inch spring-form pan. Set aside.

Beat Asiago cheese and cream cheese until smooth. Add eggs 1 at a time, beating well after each addition. Add garlic and tarragon, and combine well. Add salt and pepper to taste. Pour into prepared pan and bake for 45 minutes to 1 hour. Cake should be firm, golden and puffed. Let stand for 30 minutes before removing from pan and cutting. Serve with a lightly dressed salad.

Many colorful stories from the Prohibition era abound. The local pharmacy was licensed to prescribe alcohol, which it distributed......through the Woman's Club!

Fettuccine with Chicken and Mushrooms

Serves 4 to 5.

1	**pound boneless, skinless chicken breasts, cubed**
4	**tablespoons butter**
½	**pound mushrooms, sliced**
2	**cloves garlic, minced**
1	**large shallot, finely chopped**
¼	**cup white wine**
1	**cup chicken stock**
1	**pound fresh fettuccine**
2	**tablespoons olive oil**
1	**tablespoon fresh tarragon leaves, minced**
3	**green onions**
2	**tablespoons pine nuts**

Dash of lemon juice

Salt and pepper

Bring 1½ quarts of water to boil. Sauté diced chicken in butter. Add mushrooms, garlic and shallots. Stir a little bit. Add wine to deglaze the pan. Pour in chicken stock. At the same time put pasta into boiling water to cook for about 3 minutes. Add olive oil to the pan with chicken and mushrooms. Add fresh tarragon, green onions, pine nuts and lemon juice. Add salt and pepper to taste. Drain the pasta and mix with chicken and mushroom mixture. Serve immediately.

Chicken Artichoke Lasagna

Serves 8 to 10.

14 **tablespoons butter, divided**

1 **cup flour**

4 **cups whole milk**

Dash nutmeg

Salt and white pepper

1 **chicken, poached, with meat removed from bones**

3 **6-ounce jars marinated artichokes**

2 **13¾-ounce cans artichoke hearts**

1½ **cups Parmesan cheese, divided**

1 **pound fresh lasagna pasta**

½ **cup bread crumbs**

To make sauce, melt ½ cup butter in saucepan. Stir in flour and cook 1 minute. Slowly whisk in milk, cooking until smooth and thickened. Season with nutmeg, salt and pepper. Coarsely chop chicken and add to sauce. Drain and coarsely chop artichokes. Add artichokes and 1 cup Parmesan to sauce. Cover bottom of 12-inch x 9-inch pan with ½ cup sauce. Line with lasagna, letting noodles overhang on long edges. Cover with half of sauce. Fit in another layer of noodles and cover with remaining sauce. Cover with another layer of noodles and overlap noodles from the long edges. Cover with bread crumbs and drizzle with 6 tablespoons melted butter. Sprinkle with remaining ½ cup cheese. Bake at 350 degrees for 30 minutes. Cool 10 to 15 minutes before serving.

Note that fresh pasta does not have to be precooked. You can substitute 1½ pounds mushrooms, sautéed, for the artichokes.

Spinach Lasagna with Marinara Sauce

Serves 8 to 10.

1	pound package wide lasagna noodles
Salt	
1	pound ricotta cheese
1	egg
½	cup chopped parsley
½	cup chopped basil
1	teaspoon salt
1	tablespoon pepper
5	cloves garlic, sliced
1	tablespoon olive oil
8	cups fresh spinach
Marinara Sauce (about 3 cups)	
½	pound mozzarella cheese
Parmesan cheese to taste	

Boil water with salt and add lasagna noodles, one at a time, to the boiling water. Mix occasionally to keep them from sticking to each other. Boil for about 8 minutes until al dente. Lay noodles on aluminum foil to cool.

Mix together ricotta, egg, parsley, basil, salt and pepper. Sauté garlic in olive oil for about 3 minutes. Add spinach and sauté for another 3 minutes. Remove from heat and chop spinach.

Place a thin layer of marinara sauce on bottom of lasagna pan. Layer noodles, spinach-ricotta mixture and small amount of marinara sauce. Repeat with 2 or 3 layers ending with layer of noodles and marinara sauce. Top off with mozzarella cheese. Cook covered with aluminum foil in a preheated oven at 350 degrees for about 45 minutes. Remove foil for last 10 minutes. Cut in squares. Pass Parmesan cheese.

Marinara Sauce

Makes 4 cups sauce.

3	tablespoons olive oil
2	yellow onions, chopped
12	garlic cloves, 10 chopped and 2 whole
3	16-ounce cans crushed tomatoes
1	6-ounce can tomato puree
1	cup chopped parsley
½	cup chopped basil and 3 whole basil leaves
2	bay leaves
1	tablespoon black pepper
2	teaspoons salt
½	cup red wine

Sauté onion in oil in saucepan until onion is translucent. Add garlic. Sauté for a few minutes. Add tomatoes and tomato puree. When sauce is bubbling, add parsley, basil, bay leaves, pepper and salt. Reduce heat to simmer. Add wine and simmer for 2 hours with lid on. If sauce is too thin, remove lid for last 30 minutes.

Lasagna Rolls

A new twist on lasagna, which can be made ahead,
refrigerated overnight, and baked later.

Serves 8.

1	pound package curly-edged lasagna
1	egg, beaten
1	pound ricotta cheese
8	ounces mozzarella cheese, shredded
2	tablespoons salad oil
2	onions, chopped
2	large cloves garlic, minced
1	pound ground beef
1	cup plus 2 tablespoons chopped fresh parsley, divided
1	teaspoon basil
¾	teaspoon salt
½	teaspoon oregano
¼	teaspoon pepper
2	15½-ounce jars home-style spaghetti sauce or your favorite homemade sauce
2	tablespoons butter
2	tablespoons flour
1½	cups milk
1	cup plus 2 tablespoons grated Parmesan cheese, divided
½	teaspoon salt
¼	teaspoon pepper

Cook lasagna about 10 minutes, until tender but still firm. Rinse lasagna strips in cold water to stop further cooking. Drain and lay strips side by side on a towel.

In a bowl combine beaten egg with ricotta and mozzarella. Set aside. Heat oil in a large skillet and sauté onions and garlic until tender. Add crumbled ground beef, and cook until browned. Drain off

Lasagna Rolls (continued)

excess fat. Stir in 1 cup of the parsley, basil, salt, oregano and pepper. Blend in egg-cheese mixture.

Pour 1 jar of the spaghetti sauce into 3-quart lasagna pan. Spread each lasagna strip with a little less than ¼ cup ground beef filling and roll up. Place in baking dish.

To make béchamel sauce, melt butter in saucepan. Stir in flour, blending until smooth. Gradually stir in milk. Cook, stirring constantly, until mixture boils and thickens. Stir in 1 cup of Parmesan cheese, salt and pepper. Spoon béchamel sauce over lasagna rolls. Pour remaining spaghetti sauce over béchamel sauce. Sprinkle top with remaining chopped parsley and Parmesan cheese. Cover with foil and bake at 400 degrees for 20 minutes. Remove foil and bake 10 minutes more until bubbly. Cool 10 minutes before serving.

Stuffed Pasta Shells

Serves 6.

1	**12-ounce package jumbo pasta shells**
½	**pound Italian sweet sausage**
1	**32-ounce jar spaghetti sauce**
2	**10-ounce packages frozen chopped spinach, thawed**
2	**eggs**
1	**pound ricotta cheese**
½	**pound mozzarella cheese, shredded**
1	**teaspoon onion salt**
1	**clove garlic, minced**
⅛	**teaspoon nutmeg**
2	**tablespoons Parmesan cheese**

Cook shells, following package directions, until they are al dente (don't overcook or they may break when stuffed). Drain in a colander, rinse with cold water, and set aside.

Split the sausage casings with a sharp knife, and peel them off. Crumble meat into a large skillet, brown over medium heat, stirring frequently. Drain off fat. Add spaghetti sauce to the browned meat. Cover pan and simmer about 15 minutes.

Place thawed spinach in a strainer and press out excess moisture. In a large bowl, beat eggs slightly. Add the chopped spinach, ricotta, mozzarella, onion salt, garlic and nutmeg. Mix until ingredients are blended.

Pour about ½ cup of the sausage and spaghetti sauce mixture into the bottom of a 3-quart casserole dish. Stuff each of the cooked shells with 2 rounded teaspoons of the spinach-cheese filling. Arrange shells in a single layer in the casserole dish. Pour over remaining sauce. Sprinkle with Parmesan cheese. Bake at 350 degrees for 30 minutes.

Spaghetti with Shrimp and Black Olives

Serves 6.

8	ounces uncooked vermicelli
⅓	cup olive oil
1½	pounds shrimp, peeled and deveined
1	cup chopped onion
3	cloves garlic, crushed
2	16-ounce cans tomatoes, chopped
2	teaspoons basil
½	teaspoon salt
¼	teaspoon pepper
½	cup chopped parsley
¾	cup sliced ripe olives
3	tablespoons Parmesan cheese

Cook vermicelli and set aside after draining. Heat oil and add shrimp, onions and garlic. Cook 5 minutes, stirring. Remove shrimp from heat and set aside. Add tomatoes, basil, salt and pepper, and bring to a boil in the same pan. Cook uncovered 7 minutes. Add vermicelli, shrimp and parsley. Toss until mixture is well coated. Transfer to a serving dish. Sprinkle with ripe olives and Parmesan cheese.

Various Pasta Sauces

Several ideas to inspire your creativity.

Serving amounts up to you.

ABRUZZI
> Pancetta ham, fresh mushrooms, porcini mushrooms and tomatoes

BOLOGNESE
> Garlic, sausage, beef, spinach, carrots and onions

CAJUN CREAM
> Butter, ham, spices, oysters and whipping cream, or ham, scallions, basil, Italian parsley, cream and pepper blend

CAPONATA
> Tomatoes, eggplant, onions and garlic

CREMA POLLO
> Chicken, rosemary and cream

FIORENTINA
> Tomato sauce with chicken livers and anchovies

GENOVESE
> Meatless tomato sauce with spinach, carrots, basil and onions

GORGONZOLA WALNUT CREAM
> Speaks for itself

PEPPERONATI
> Tangy-red, green and yellow peppers, onions, tomatoes and garlic

PUTTANESCA
> Spicy-tomatoes, anchovies, capers, black olives, garlic and red pepper flakes

QUATTRO FORMAGGI
> Blend of cheeses-talleggio, fontina, Romano cheeses and cream

Various Pasta Sauces (continued)

SAUCE SARDINIA
Red sauce with mushrooms, tomatoes, garlic and olives

SORELLO SAUCE
Light tomato sauce with anchovies, garlic and spices

SUN-DRIED TOMATO
Sun-dried tomatoes, garlic, oil and basil

TOMATO BASIL CREAM
Sautéed onions, basil, tomatoes and cream

Ziti Providence

Serves 8 to 10.

2	**pounds ground beef**
2	**cloves garlic, minced**
2	**onions, chopped**
1	**quart spaghetti sauce**
1	**pound ziti or penne pasta, cooked**
1	**pound colby or longhorn cheese, grated**
½	**pound pepperoni, sliced**
12	**ounces mozzarella cheese, grated**
½	**cup Parmesan cheese, grated**

Brown ground beef, garlic and onions together. Add spaghetti sauce. Spread cooked ziti in 10½-inch x 15½-inch baking pan and cover with grated colby cheese. Cover with sauce mixture, sliced pepperoni, mozzarella and Parmesan in that order. Bake in preheated oven at 325 degrees for 45 minutes or until top is browned.

Real Cajun Red Beans and Rice

Serves 6 to 8.

1	pound dried red beans
2	quarts water
3	cups chopped onions
1	bunch green onions, chopped
1	cup chopped parsley
1	cup chopped bell pepper
2	cloves garlic, crushed
1	tablespoon salt
1	teaspoon cayenne pepper
1	teaspoon black pepper
3	generous dashes Tabasco sauce
1	tablespoon Worcestershire sauce
1	4-ounce can tomato sauce
¼	teaspoon oregano
¾	teaspoon dried thyme
1	pound smoked sausage, sliced

Cooked rice

Soak beans in a lot of water overnight. Drain. Cook beans in 2 quarts water at low heat slowly for 45 minutes. Add onions, parsley, bell pepper, garlic, salt, cayenne, black pepper, Tabasco, Worcestershire, tomato sauce, oregano and thyme. Cook at low heat 1 hour and 45 minutes, stirring occasionally. Add sausage, if used, for the last 45 minutes. Cool and let stand. Add more salt, if needed. Reheat and bring to a boil, then lower heat and simmer 30 to 40 minutes. Serve over boiled or steamed rice.

Savory Black Bean Pancakes

Serve as part of meatless meal for breakfast or supper with yogurt and salsa.

Serves 4 to 5.

1	**15-ounce can black beans**
2	**eggs**
1	**cup buttermilk**
1	**cup flour**
1	**tablespoon sugar**
1½	**teaspoons baking powder**
¾	**teaspoon baking soda**
½	**teaspoon salt**
1	**cup yogurt or sour cream**
1	**cup salsa**

Drain the black beans, rinse them, then drain well again. Puree in a food processor until smooth, then scrape the mixture into a bowl. Beat in the eggs and buttermilk.

Stir and mix together the flour, sugar, baking powder, baking soda and salt.

Add to the bean mixture and stir just until the batter is blended. Do not overbeat. Cook on a hot lightly greased griddle, cooking each pancake about 2 minutes on each side. Serve hot and pass bowls of yogurt or sour cream and salsa as an accompaniment.

Some of Sausalito's early homes were shipped around Cape Horn in sections, then reassembled on the steep and rocky hillsides.

Bobotie

Serves 4.

½	**pound ground beef**
½	**pound ground lamb**
3	**tablespoons vegetable oil**
1¾	**cups onion, finely chopped**
2	**tablespoons curry powder**
4	**large garlic cloves, minced**
¾	**cup raisins**
⅔	**cup lemon juice**
½	**cup apricot preserves**
½	**cup dried apricots, chopped**
2	**teaspoons jalapeño chiles, minced**
1	**teaspoon salt, divided**
⅔	**cup half-and-half cream**
½	**cup bread crumbs**
2	**cups milk**
4	**eggs**

Crumble lamb and beef and cook in hot oil until brown, about 5 minutes. Add onions and stir about 3 minutes. Add curry and garlic and stir about 2 minutes. Add raisins, preserves, lemon juice, dried apricots, chiles and ½ teaspoon salt. Stir until mixture thickens about 5 minutes. Mix in half-and-half and bread crumbs. Cool completely.

Preheat oven to 350 degrees. Transfer mixture to 7 x 12- inch glass casserole dish. Whisk milk, eggs and ½ teaspoon salt in bowl. Pour over meat mixture. Bake 35 to 45 minutes until custard topping has set. Serve with rice or grits.

Mr. Abdou's Special

Serves 4.

1	**eggplant**
	Olive oil
1	**pound ground round or ground lamb**
1	**onion, chopped**
4	**cloves garlic, minced**
$\frac{1}{2}$	**teaspoon cinnamon, or to taste**
$\frac{1}{2}$	**teaspoon cumin**
$\frac{1}{4}$	**teaspoon coriander**
	Salt and pepper
2	**16-ounce cans stewed tomatoes**
2	**ounces goat cheese**
$\frac{1}{4}$	**cup pine nuts**
	Cooked rice

Quarter eggplant. Salt and let sit for 40 minutes. Press water out with a paper towel. Brown on all sides in olive oil. Remove and place in a casserole dish. Sauté meat, onion and garlic until lightly browned. Add cinnamon, cumin, coriander, salt and pepper. Pour over the eggplant. Arrange tomatoes around the side. Cut or crumble goat cheese into small pieces and sprinkle over top. Bake uncovered at 350 degrees for about 45 minutes. Lightly toast pine nuts. When ready to serve, sprinkle pine nuts on top. Serve with rice.

Heidi's Bourbon Chili

*This won a prize for the Sausalito Woman's Club
at our annual local Chili Cook-Off.*

Serves 20.

8	pounds lean beef, cubed
4	pounds pork, cubed
¼	cup oil
5	onions, chopped
6	stalks celery, diced
12	cloves garlic, minced
2	8-ounce cans tomato sauce
5	cups homemade brown stock or canned beef stock
1	cup bourbon
1	12-ounce bottle dark beer
3	tablespoons cumin
1	tablespoon oregano
1	teaspoon nutmeg
1	tablespoon sugar
6	tablespoons chili powder
1	teaspoon mace
5	teaspoons chili flakes
2	tablespoons unsweetened cocoa or 2 chocolate squares

Salt and pepper

5	cups cooked pinto, pink or kidney beans
1	bunch cilantro, chopped
1	onion, chopped
1	pound sharp cheddar cheese, grated

In a large Dutch oven brown beef and pork in oil. Transfer meat into a large stock pot. In the same Dutch oven sauté onion, celery and garlic until soft. Add vegetables to meat. Stir in tomato sauce, beef stock and bourbon. Add beer, cumin, oregano, nutmeg, sugar,

Heidi's Bourbon Chili (continued)

chili powder, mace, chili flakes, cocoa powder, salt and pepper and stir. Simmer uncovered for 2½ to 3 hours. If more liquid is needed add water or more beer or bourbon.

Serve with pinto, pink or kidney beans. Purists always add a few beans on top. Let your fellow diners choose. Garnish with chopped cilantro. Serve with bowls of chopped onion and grated cheese to sprinkle on top.

Rich Brown Stock

Makes 3 quarts.

- **10 pounds beef bones**
- **1 pound onions**
- **1 pound carrots**
- **2 leeks**
- **2 stalks celery**
- **3 quarts water**
- **8 peppercorns**
- **2 bay leaves**
- **1 sprig thyme**

Roast beef bones at 450 degrees for 45 minutes. Add bones, onions, carrots, leeks, celery, and water in stock pot. Make bouquet garni from peppercorns, bay leaves, and thyme by tying seasoning in a small piece of cheesecloth. Add to pot. Simmer 8 to 10 hours. Remove bouquet garni.

Chicken Enchilada Bake with Mushroom Sauce

A hearty meal and only 239 calories per serving!

Serves 8.

2	poblano chiles, cut in half and seeded
2	Anaheim chiles, cut in half and seeded
1	red bell pepper, cut in half and seeded
1	tablespoon olive oil
3	cups cremini mushrooms, sliced
½	cup shiitake or portobello mushrooms, sliced
½	cup green onions, sliced
4	cloves garlic, minced
2	tablespoons flour
½	teaspoon sage
¼	teaspoon cumin
¼	cup cilantro, chopped
¼	teaspoon black pepper
1¼	cups chicken broth
½	cup water
4	ounces non-fat cream cheese
	Cooking spray
9	corn tortillas, cut in half
2¼	cups cooked, boneless, skinned and shredded chicken breast meat
¼	cup Parmesan, Asiago and/or Romano cheese, grated
½	cup low-fat Jack cheese, shredded

Place chiles and pepper skin side up on a cookie sheet. Broil 5 minutes until blackened. Sweat in plastic or paper bag for 15 minutes. Remove blackened skin and chop.

Heat oil in nonstick skillet. Add mushrooms, onion, and garlic. Sauté 5 minutes. Stir in flour, sage, cumin, cilantro and black pepper. Cook

Chicken Enchilada Bake (continued)

2 minutes. Stir in chiles, broth, water and simmer 5 minutes, stirring constantly. Stir in cream cheese. Remove from heat.

Preheat oven to 350 degrees. Coat oblong baking dish with cooking spray. Spoon 1 cup sauce into dish and layer 6 half tortillas, ¾ cup chicken meat and ⅓ of the cheeses on top. Repeat the layers 2 more times. Bake for 35 minutes.

A great make-ahead company dish or an easy one to put together and deliver to a friend.

California Gumbo

Lots of good parties have featured these 2 excellent gumbos.
We couldn't decide on our favorite so we included both.

Serves 10 to 12.

1½ **cups flour**

1 **teaspoon salt**

2 **teaspoons dried garlic**

2 **teaspoons black pepper**

½ **teaspoon cayenne pepper**

3-4 **pounds chicken parts, skinned and boned**

Vegetable oil

1½ **cups onion, finely chopped**

1½ **cups green bell pepper, finely diced**

1½ **cups celery, finely diced**

¼ **cup garlic, minced**

4 **cups chicken stock**

1 **teaspoon thyme**

3 **tablespoons Worcestershire sauce**

3 **bay leaves**

1 **teaspoon paprika**

1 **tablespoon sugar**

1 **pound smoked pork sausage, sliced into rounds**

3 **cups chopped okra**

1 **tablespoon file powder, dissolved in cold water**

2 **pounds medium prawns, peeled**

White rice, cooked

In a bag mix flour, salt, garlic, black pepper and cayenne pepper. Cut boned chicken into 1 to 2-inch cubes and shake in bag to coat. Remove excess flour and let pieces stand for 30 minutes. Save ½ cup of the flour mixture for the roux. In a large pot, brown chicken on all sides in 1-inch vegetable oil. Drain on paper towels and keep warm.

California Gumbo (continued)

Remove all oil except ½ cup. Scrape all brown bits from bottom of pan. Add ½ cup flour mixture. Cook, stirring constantly, until roux is dark brown. Do not burn. Add onions, bell pepper, celery and garlic. Stir and cook until vegetables are soft. Add chicken stock gradually while stirring until thickened. Return chicken to mixture with thyme, Worcestershire, bay leaves, paprika, sugar, smoked pork sausage and okra.

Simmer for 45 to 60 minutes, adding chicken broth as needed until chicken is tender. Add file powder and cook until blended. Refrigerate gumbo several hours or overnight.

Just before serving bring to a simmer and add prawns. Cook about 5 to 10 minutes or until prawns turn pink. Gumbo is a thick soup and should be served over rice in a soup bowl.

Chicken, Sausage and Shrimp Gumbo

Serves 4.

1	onion, chopped
½	green bell pepper, diced
1	stalk celery, diced
2	garlic cloves, minced
6-8	ounces hot or mild sausage, crumbled
2½	tablespoons oil, divided
1	quart chicken stock
2	tablespoons flour
½	red bell pepper, diced
1	cup tomatoes, diced
½	teaspoon thyme
⅛	teaspoon cayenne pepper
⅛	teaspoon black pepper
¼	teaspoon white pepper
½	teaspoon salt
½	roasted chicken, meat removed and cubed
3	ounces okra, sliced
½-1	teaspoon file powder, to taste
½	pound rock shrimp

Cooked white rice

Green onions, sliced thin

Tabasco sauce

Sauté onion, green pepper, celery, garlic and sausage in 1 tablespoon oil in a large ovenproof stockpot or casserole until onions are softened and bits of sausage are lightly browned. Drain off fat. Add stock and simmer while preparing rest of gumbo.

To make roux, heat 1½ tablespoons oil over medium-low heat. Sprinkle in flour, stirring constantly until mixture takes on a nutty brown color. Stir roux into simmering soup. Add red bell pepper,

Chicken, Sausage and Shrimp Gumbo (continued)

tomatoes, thyme, all peppers and salt. Simmer until slightly thickened. Add chicken, okra and file powder. Simmer a few minutes longer, until okra is cooked through. Remove from oven and let cool. Refrigerate overnight to blend flavors. Reheat in low oven at 250 degrees for 2 hours. Remove from oven, add rock shrimp and bring to boil on stovetop. Serve each portion ladled over scoop of rice. Garnish with green onions. Pass Tabasco sauce at table.

Seafood Risotto

Serves 4.

½	**pound bay scallops**
1	**cup orange juice**
½	**pound medium shrimp**
1	**cup grapefruit juice**
¼	**cup butter**
2	**shallots, minced**
1	**cup Arborio rice**
2	**cups simmering chicken stock**
2	**tablespoon olive oil**
⅛	**pound brown mushrooms, sliced**
¼	**cup Parmesan cheese**
2	**tablespoons parsley, minced**

Marinate scallops in orange juice and shrimp in grapefruit juice for 30 minutes. Sauté shallots 5 minutes in butter. Add rice and sauté. Add ¼ cup stock, stirring constantly, until absorbed. Continue to add ¼ cup stock at a time, cooking thoroughly after each addition, for about 18 to 20 minutes total cooking time. Sauté scallops, shrimp and mushrooms in olive oil for 2 to 3 minutes. Add to risotto, stir in cheese and parsley. Serve immediately.

Polenta Sandwich

Serves 4.

2	cloves garlic, minced
2	tablespoons balsamic vinegar
¼	cup olive oil
½	teaspoon black pepper
½	teaspoon chopped fresh thyme
1	small eggplant, cut into 8 slices
1	pound cooked polenta, cut into 8 slices ½-inch thick
⅓	cup soft goat cheese
8	slices mozzarella cheese

Fresh tomato sauce (recipe follows)

Chives, chopped

Basil, chopped

Asiago cheese

Mix together garlic, vinegar, olive oil, pepper and thyme. Marinate eggplant slices in this mixture for at least 1 hour. Place marinated eggplant on cookie sheet sprayed with oil. Bake at 350 degrees for about 20 minutes, until soft and brown.

Assemble each sandwich as follows: 1 slice polenta, 2 teaspoons goat cheese, 1 slice eggplant, 1 slice mozzarella. Place stacks in baking pan and bake at 350 degrees for 20 minutes. Serve hot on a bed of your own fresh tomato sauce. Sprinkle with fresh chives and basil. Pass fresh Asiago cheese.

Fresh Tomato Sauce

3   **tablespoons olive oil**
4   **cloves garlic, chopped**
1   **onion, chopped**
6-8 **tomatoes, skinned, seeded and chopped**
1   **pinch red pepper flakes**
1   **bay leaf**
½   **cup chopped fresh basil**
Salt and freshly ground pepper

In olive oil gently sauté garlic, onion, tomatoes, red pepper flakes, bay leaf, basil, salt and pepper. Cook 30 minutes. Press through food mill, or leave chunky.

Paella

A great party dish.

Serves 8.

1	teaspoon paprika
1	tablespoon grated fresh ginger

Salt and pepper

2	chickens, cut up, or 16 to 20 chicken parts
½	pound bacon, diced
½	cup olive oil
1½	pounds shrimp, peeled, or 2 small lobsters, shelled
2	onions, chopped
2	green peppers, diced
6	cloves garlic, minced
3	tomatoes, peeled and cut in pieces
1	16-ounce can artichoke hearts, drained
2	cups long grain rice
1½	cups bottled clam juice
1½-2	cups chicken broth
1	8-ounce can minced clams with juice
12	1-inch pieces chorizo sausage
½	teaspoon powdered saffron
½	cup white wine

Rub paprika, ginger, salt and pepper on chicken. In a heavy iron skillet cook bacon until crisp. Remove bacon and fat and add oil. When sizzling, add chicken pieces and sauté until golden brown. Remove chicken and keep warm. Sauté shrimp until just pink. Remove and keep warm. Sauté onions, green peppers and garlic. Add tomatoes and artichoke hearts and cook 5 minutes. Add rice. Cook, stirring occasionally until rice takes on some color. Return chicken, bacon and seafood to skillet. Add clam juice and 1½ cups chicken broth. Cover and bake 15 minutes at 350 degrees until chicken is almost tender. Add minced clams, sausage, saffron, seafood and white wine. (Can be done to this point, then refrigerated and finished baking just before serving.) Cover and bake until tender, adding more hot chicken broth as needed.

Spicy Shrimp in Tortillas
A Mexican beer is wonderful with this meal.

Serves 2.

6	**flour tortillas**
1	**medium onion, chopped**
1	**large garlic clove, minced**
2	**tablespoons oil**
2	**tomatoes, chopped**
1	**fresh jalapeño, minced, or** **4-ounce can chopped chiles**
3	**tablespoons lime juice**
2	**tablespoons cilantro, chopped**
½	**teaspoon salt**
½	**pound medium shrimp, shelled**
1	**small avocado**
2	**heaping tablespoons sour cream**
1	**lime, cut in wedges**
2	**green onions, thinly sliced**

Wrap tortillas in aluminum foil and heat in 300 degree oven. Cook onion and garlic in hot oil until tender. Add tomatoes and chiles. Cook, stirring gently, until most of the liquid evaporates. Add lime juice, cilantro, and salt. Add shrimp and cook until pink.

Working with one tortilla at a time, spoon some of the sautéed shrimp onto one quarter of a warm tortilla. Fold in half, and then again in half, making a triangular package. To serve, overlap three tortillas on a plate. Garnish with a slice of avocado, sour cream, a few lime wedges and scatter with sliced green onions.

Curried Vegetables and Rice

A great vegetarian dish. This makes tons, so serve at a buffet or freeze it in individual packets for later use.

Serves 10 to 12.

2   15-ounce cans pinto beans
2   15-ounce cans garbanzo beans
3   tablespoons vegetable oil
½   cup mustard seeds
1   teaspoon cinnamon
1   teaspoon cardamom
1   teaspoon cumin
2   tablespoons curry powder
10 cloves garlic, minced
1   tablespoon minced fresh ginger
2   large onions, thinly sliced
1   28-ounce can tomatoes, cut up
1   yam, peeled and diced
8   carrots, peeled and sliced
4   zucchini, diced

Drain pinto and garbanzo beans. Heat oil in large pan. Add mustard seeds and cook until they pop. Add spices and cook 2 minutes. Add garlic, ginger and onions and cook on low heat about 15 minutes, until soft. Add tomatoes, yam and carrots and simmer 30 minutes. Add pinto and garbanzo beans and zucchini and simmer another 20 minutes. Serve over rice.

Meat, Seafood and Poultry

The Sausalito Art Festival

Sausalito's reputation as an art community is reaffirmed every Labor Day weekend when an annual art festival attracts upwards of 40,000 visitors, and consumes the time and energy of many residents.

From rather modest beginnings in 1952 (it was held on a beach in conjunction with a local salmon derby), the festival is now considered one of the most prestigious art shows in America. More than 200 juried entrants from across the country are showcased at the three-day event. While superb fine arts and crafts are the core of the festival, much more happens on the grounds. Top musical entertainment is a daily feature, a whole area is devoted to children's activities, fine wines are offered for tasting, and there are treats galore in the Gourmet Food Court. Members of local volunteer organizations, including the Sausalito Woman's Club, run the food booths as fundraisers.

The festival is truly a community affair. Some 1,200 volunteers are needed to fill the myriad tasks that make the weekend a success - starting with the Blue Ribbon Garbage Committee whose members keep the area tidy. Whether a participant or a patron, it's a weekend not to be missed in the Sausalito yearly calendar.

By Bea Seidler

Barbecued Steak

Serves 6 to 8.

3-4 pounds boneless beef top sirloin or top round steak

MARINADE

½ **medium onion, cut into quarters**

¼ **cup honey**

¼ **cup fresh lime juice**

10-20 **quarter-size slices fresh ginger**

1-2 **jalapeño peppers, cut in half**

3 **cloves garlic**

½ **teaspoon ground allspice**

½ **teaspoon paprika**

½ **teaspoon dried thyme leaves**

Mix marinade ingredients in blender or food processor. Put beef steak and marinade in zip-top plastic bag, turning to coat. Close bag securely and marinate in refrigerator 1 to 2 hours, turning once.

Remove steak from plastic bag, reserving marinade. Barbecue until desired doneness. In a small saucepan bring marinade to a rolling boil over high heat. Boil 2 minutes; strain and use for sauce. Cut steak into thin slices and arrange on serving platter. Serve with sauce.

The passage of the Woman's Suffrage Act in 1920 brought about many positive changes. The Sausalito Woman's Club began to participate actively in local politics, worked to bring adequate street lighting to the city, and helped to focus attention on effective law enforcement in the town.

Smothered Flank Steak

Very, very spicy and hot!

Serves 4.

SEASONING MIX

2	teaspoons salt
1½	teaspoons onion powder
1½	teaspoons garlic powder
1¼	teaspoons paprika
1	teaspoon dried chervil
¾	teaspoon dry mustard
½	teaspoon black pepper
½	teaspoon white pepper
½	teaspoon cayenne pepper
½	teaspoon ground cumin

STEAK AND SAUCE

1	pound flank steak, cut in ¼-inch thin, diagonal slices
2	cups chopped onions
1½	cups chopped green bell peppers
1½	cups chopped celery
5	cups chicken or beef stock
6	tablespoons flour

Combine the seasoning mix ingredients. For less heat, reduce cayenne pepper. Rub 2 tablespoons of the seasoning mix on steak slices. Brown on all sides in a preheated 5 quart nonstick pot. Remove steak and add the onions, bell peppers, celery and remaining seasoning mix. Cook 2 minutes. Stir in 1 cup of stock and cook until vegetables start to brown about 10 minutes. Toast flour in a separate skillet, low heat, until a nutty brown color, being careful to stir and prevent burning. Add the browned flour and mix until paste forms. Add 3 cups stock and steak. Bring to boil. Simmer until sauce is thick. Add remaining stock and continue to cook until steak is tender about 30 minutes. Serve over rice, pasta or potatoes.

Barbecue Beef Sandwiches

This was a big hit at one of our Rotary Lunches.

Serves 8 to 10.

2	tablespoons salad oil
4-5	pounds cross-rib or sirloin tip roast or boneless loin pork roast
2	large onions, chopped
1	large green pepper, seeded and chopped
2	stalks celery, chopped
2	large cloves garlic, minced
1	cup catsup
1	1-pound can stewed tomatoes
¼	cup cider vinegar
⅓	cup brown sugar, firmly packed
1	teaspoon chili powder
½	teaspoon dry basil
½	teaspoon dry oregano
½	teaspoon ground cinnamon
½	teaspoon liquid smoke, optional

Salt and pepper
8-10 onion rolls

Heat oil in a 6 to 8 quart casserole. Brown meat; remove and set aside. Add onions, green pepper, celery and garlic. Cook until onions are limp. Add catsup, tomatoes, vinegar, brown sugar, chili powder, basil, oregano, cinnamon, salt, pepper and liquid smoke. Simmer uncovered for about 10 minutes. Return meat to pan; spoon sauce over it. Cover and bake at 325 degrees for about 3 hours until meat is tender. Refrigerate.

Remove fat. Thinly slice meat and return to pan. Cover and heat at 350 degrees for about 55 minutes. Spoon meat and sauce onto onion rolls to serve.

Company Meatloaf

This recipe also makes great meatballs.

Serves 6 to 8 hearty eaters.

1   **pound ground beef**
½   **pound ground veal**
½   **pound ground pork**
1   **cup milk**
3   **slices white or wheat toast**
Salt and pepper to taste
1   **tablespoon butter**
2   **tablespoons cooking oil**
1   **onion, chopped fine**
1   **clove garlic, minced**
1   **green pepper, chopped**
¼   **cup fresh parsley, minced**
Juice of ½ lemon
1   **tablespoon Worcestershire sauce**
1   **tablespoon Dijon mustard**
1   **teaspoon salt**
1   **cup grated Parmesan cheese**
2   **eggs**

Put meat in a large mixing bowl; put the milk in a different bowl. Trim crusts off toast and crumble slices into milk. Mash the toast until blended with milk. Add this mixture to the meat with salt and pepper and mix well.

Put butter and oil in a skillet and sauté onion, garlic and green pepper until limp. Add the parsley, lemon juice, Worcestershire sauce, mustard and salt and stir. Turn into the meat mixture. Add cheese and eggs and mix thoroughly. Rub a loaf pan with cooking oil and pack the meat mixture into the pan. Bake at 350 degrees for 1 hour until loaf has a glaze on top and draws away from the edges of pan. Serve with horseradish, if desired.

Company Meatloaf (continued)

For meatballs: Form meat mixture into balls and brown in a small amount of olive oil. Cover with ½ cup chicken stock, ½ cup white wine, salt and pepper. Cover and simmer 30 minutes. Top with chopped Italian parsley and sliced mushrooms the last 15 minutes.

Zegadine Goulash

Serves 4 to 6.

3	**tablespoons Wondra flour**
3	**tablespoons paprika**
Salt and pepper	
2	**pounds boneless veal, cut in 1½-inch cubes**
3	**tablespoons oil**
2	**cups sliced onions**
1	**cup stewed tomatoes**
1	**cup sauerkraut**
1	**tablespoon Worcestershire sauce**
⅓	**cup water**
½	**cup sour cream**
1	**pound noodles boiled**

Put flour and paprika in a paper bag with salt and pepper to taste. Put 6 pieces of veal in at a time and shake to coat. Brown veal and onions in oil. Add tomatoes, sauerkraut, Worcestershire sauce and water. Bake at 325 degrees for 2 hours. Remove from oven and stir in sour cream until smooth. Serve over boiled noodles.

Belgian Beef and Carrot Stew

Serve with a green salad and lots of fresh sourdough bread,
since this is what the Belgians call a mopping stew.

Serves 8.

4	pounds stewing beef, cut in bite-size pieces
1	bottle (750 ml.) of red wine, reserve ¼ cup
6-8	whole cloves
¼	pound bacon
1	tablespoon olive oil
30	small white onions
12	large carrots, peeled and cut into rounds
1	tablespoon tomato paste
1	teaspoon powdered orange peel
1	teaspoon dried thyme
1	dried bay leaf
1	teaspoon salt
½	teaspoon pepper
1	heaping tablespoon cornstarch

Marinate beef overnight in wine and clove mixture.

Cut bacon into ¼ inch squares and boil for 5 minutes. Drain and dry. Fry in olive oil until lightly browned. Place in large stew pot. Brown beef on high heat in the same frying pan. Add to stew pot. Drop the white onions in boiling water for a few seconds to make peeling them easy. Add peeled onions and carrots to pot. Add wine marinade, tomato paste, orange peel, thyme, bay, salt and pepper. Bring to a simmer on top of stove; cover and put in a preheated 350 degree oven. Cook for 1 to 1½ hours. When cooked, add cornstarch to reserved ¼ cup red wine, mixing thoroughly, and add to stew to thicken sauce.

Zesty Veal Strips

*Thin strips of veal sautéed with dried
mushrooms make this a quick, low-fat and satisfying meal.*

Serves 2 to 3.

1	**pound veal scaloppine**
½	**pound zucchini**
1	**ounce dried mushrooms**
2	**tablespoons vegetable oil**
1	**clove garlic, minced**
1	**8-ounce can tomato sauce**
2	**tablespoons lemon juice**
¼	**cup muscat wine or sherry**
½	**teaspoon thyme**
½	**teaspoon oregano**
Salt and pepper	
2	**tablespoons chopped parsley**

Cut veal into strips ½-inch wide. Cut zucchini into strips the same size as veal. Soak mushrooms in warm water to cover for 10 minutes; drain and slice into strips.

In a large skillet heat oil and add zucchini strips and garlic. Sauté about 2 minutes. Add veal strips and sauté, stirring constantly, until lightly browned on all sides. Add mushroom strips and sauté another 1 to 2 minutes. Add tomato sauce, lemon juice, wine, thyme, oregano, salt and pepper. Simmer for 5 minutes. Serve at once, sprinkled with parsley. Serve with rice or pasta.

Worry-Free Rare Roast Beef

This works every time!

Serves 4 to 8.

1   roast beef, bone in, any size

In the morning take roast out of the refrigerator and let stand for 1 hour. Preheat oven to 375 degrees. Put roast in the oven and cook for 1 hour. Turn off the heat, but leave roast in the oven. <u>Do</u> <u>not</u> open the door and do not use a meat thermometer. Thirty minutes before serving, but no longer than 6 hours after you turned off the oven, turn the oven back on to 375 degrees. Every slice will be perfect-uniformly pink. If you like your beef less rare, simply increase the cooking time at the end in small increments (10 minutes). You will become courageous as you practice.

Marinated Lamb Chops

This received rave reviews at one of our progressive dinners.

Serves 4.

¾	**cup balsamic vinegar**
6	**tablespoons olive oil**
3	**tablespoons lemon juice**
3	**tablespoons fresh rosemary, or 3 teaspoons dry**
6	**cloves garlic, minced**
1	**teaspoon black pepper**
8	**1-inch thick lamb chops**

Mix together vinegar, oil, lemon juice, rosemary, garlic and pepper. Marinate lamb chops for about 4 hours. Grill covered for 5 to 6 minutes per side on hot grill. Baste frequently.

Mexican Style Leg of Lamb

Serves 8 to 10.

5-6 **pound leg of lamb**
1 **cup dry red wine**
½ **cup orange juice**
¼ **cup chili sauce**
2 **tablespoons olive oil**
¼ **cup water**
1 **onion, finely chopped**
2 **cloves garlic, minced**
1 **tablespoon oregano**
1 **teaspoon cumin**
1 **tablespoon brown sugar**
Salt and pepper to taste

Place meat in as small a glass casserole dish as will fit. Combine remaining ingredients and pour over meat. Refrigerate overnight, turning occasionally. Remove meat from marinade and drain, reserving marinade. Place in roasting pan and roast at 450 degrees for 15 minutes. Reduce heat to 350 degrees and pour marinade over meat. Continue cooking, basting frequently, for about 2½ hours or until meat is tender. Add more liquid to pan juices, if needed. Serve remaining juices with meat. Serve with pilaf or potatoes.

Lamb Sauté

Serves 4.

8	**loin lamb chops or boneless slices of lamb about 1 inch thick**

Flour

Salt

Few grinds fresh pepper

1	**egg**
2	**teaspoons olive oil**
¼	**teaspoon dried thyme**
½	**cup fresh bread crumbs, white or French bread**
2	**tablespoons freshly grated Parmesan cheese**
2	**teaspoons unsalted butter or olive oil**
1-2	**teaspoons lemon juice**

Watercress or parsley

Trim chops or lamb slices of all fat. Mix flour with salt and pepper and dust the lamb pieces lightly, shaking off the excess. Beat the egg with olive oil and thyme. Mix the bread crumbs and Parmesan cheese. Dip the lamb pieces into the egg mixture and then into the bread crumb mixture to coat. Set aside on waxed paper. Heat 2 teaspoons unsalted butter or oil, or both, in a large, nonstick skillet and add the lamb pieces. Sauté the lamb for 6 to 8 minutes or until the crumbs are golden on the outside and lamb is rare inside. Deglaze the pan with lemon juice and pour over the lamb. Garnish with watercress or parsley.

Roasted Lamb
with Aromatic Couscous

*The combination of cumin, basil and mint lends an aromatic,
Near Eastern quality to lamb. Quickly cooked vegetables complement a
bed of soft, nutty couscous, which soaks up the rich tomato-based sauce.*

Serves 4.

4	cups water
1	teaspoon salt
2	cups instant couscous
8	lamb chops

Salt and pepper

1	small red onion, sliced
2	medium zucchini, cut in ¼-inch slices

Cumin powder

2	garlic cloves, minced
1	14½-ounce can ready cut tomatoes
1	15-ounce can cannellini beans, drained
1	cup chicken broth
¼	cup fresh basil, finely chopped
2	tablespoons fresh mint, finely chopped

Bring water and salt to a boil in medium saucepan. Add the couscous.
Turn off heat, cover and let sit while preparing lamb. Season chops
with salt and pepper. Place chops in preheated nonstick skillet and
sear briefly on each side. Remove lamb to roasting pan and roast at
400 degrees for 6 to 10 minutes. Add the onion and zucchini to the
skillet. Sauté for 2 to 3 minutes, stirring well and seasoning lightly
with cumin, salt and pepper. Add the garlic, tomatoes, beans, chicken
broth and basil. Reduce heat to low and cover, simmer for 3 minutes.
Just before serving stir in the mint. Divide the couscous among 4 soup
plates. Top with bean-tomato mixture and lamb chops.

Lamb Saté

Far Eastern version of skewered, barbecued lamb.

Serves 6 to 8.

MARINADE

1	tablespoon ground coriander
½	teaspoon pepper
1	onion, chopped
2	cloves garlic
½	cup soy sauce
½	cup lemon juice

Juice of 1 orange

½	cup peanut butter
¼	cup brown sugar
½	cup salad oil

Dash of cayenne

Few drops of Tabasco

1	leg of lamb, boned and cubed
8	small zucchini, sliced 1-inch thick
16	small white onions, peeled
2	bell peppers, cut into 1-inch squares

Mix together marinade ingredients. Pour over meat and marinate over-night. Soak wooden skewers for at least 15 minutes before using. Put meat on skewers, alternating with zucchini, onions and bell peppers. Brush with sauce while barbecuing to desired doneness. Bring remaining marinade to a boil for I minute and serve in bowl at table.

Lamb Stew

Serves 4 to 6.

3   **pounds lamb stew meat with bone, or
2 pounds boneless**

2½   **tablespoons olive oil**

¾   **cup sliced onions**

2   **large cloves garlic, sliced**

1   **1¼-pound can tomatoes**

1   **pound sliced mushrooms**

1-3 **teaspoons oregano**

Salt and pepper to taste

⅔   **cup red wine**

In a heavy skillet or Dutch oven, heat oil and add lamb. Cook until lightly brown on all sides. Add all other ingredients except wine. Cook over low heat for 35 to 40 minutes, or until lamb is tender. Add wine and cook another 20 to 30 minutes. Serve with pasta or rice.

For variety add any of the following vegetables: string beans, carrots, potatoes, cubed eggplant, okra or zucchini.

Moroccan Lamb
with Onions and Prunes

Orange flower water is available in drug or liquor stores.

Serves 8.

8   lamb shanks or 4 pounds lean, boneless lamb
     cut into 1-inch pieces
1½   teaspoons saffron
1½   teaspoons cinnamon
1   teaspoon ground ginger
5   cups cold water
6   tablespoons honey, divided
2   pounds small white onions, trimmed and peeled
1   cup dried prunes
1   tablespoon orange flower water
3   tablespoons toasted sesame seeds
Rice or couscous

Preheat oven to 350 degrees. In a large, heavy casserole, combine the lamb, saffron, cinnamon, ginger, water and 3 tablespoons honey. The liquid should cover the lamb halfway; add more water if necessary. Bring to a boil over high heat, stirring occasionally. Reduce heat and simmer, covered for 35 minutes. Remove from heat and drain liquid to a saucepan. Boil briskly, uncovered, until it is reduced to 3 cups. Pour liquid back into casserole. Add onions, prunes and orange flower water and remaining 3 tablespoons honey. Cover and bake in oven for 45 minutes, or until lamb and onions are brown and tender and liquid is almost evaporated. Transfer to a platter and sprinkle with toasted sesame seeds. Serve with rice or couscous.

Succulent Roast Pork with Fennel

This recipe can be served hot or at room temperature (cucina fresca) which is great on a picnic or a deck overlooking San Francisco Bay.

Serves 6 to 8.

6	**cloves garlic, minced**
2	**tablespoons fennel seeds**
2	**teaspoons coarse salt**
	Freshly ground pepper
4	**pounds boneless pork rib roast**
	Olive oil

Make a paste with the garlic, fennel, salt and pepper in a mortar and pestle (or mash with the side of a chef's knife). Unroll the roast and spread most of the paste over the meat, reserving 1 tablespoon. Roll meat so that the darker meat surrounds the white tenderloin and then tie it up. Make a few ½-inch incisions in the meat and stuff some of the paste into them. Rub remaining over all. Rub a little oil over the meat and roast, uncovered, in a preheated 350 degree oven about 2 hours, or until the internal temperature reaches 170 degrees. Baste a few times with the pan juices. Remove roast and allow to cool. Cut into ½-inch slices and drizzle a little fruity olive oil over the meat. Great with roasted potatoes.

Sausalito, with a population of about 2,000, began the incorporation process in 1893. The 1906 shake and roll of the San Francisco earthquake and fire initiated the start of building growth. When the Golden Gate Bridge connected Sausalito to San Francisco in 1937, the boom was on!

Pork Loin
with Whiskey and Prunes

This is a favorite recipe from a cooking class in Paris.

Serves 8.

4	**pounds boneless pork tenderloin roast**
1½	**cups Dijon mustard**
¾	**cup honey, divided**
1	**cup bourbon whiskey**
1½	**cups chicken stock**
1	**cup cream**
2	**cups pitted prunes**

Salt and pepper to taste

Spread pork with mustard. Place in heavy casserole on top of stove. Add half the honey and brown (using no additional fat) on all sides, being careful not to burn. Add whiskey and stock. Cover and simmer for 1 hour. Remove pork. Add remainder of honey and the cream, reducing to thicken sauce. Soak prunes in hot water for 20 minutes. 10 minutes before serving, add prunes and season with salt and pepper. Slice pork and serve on a warm platter with the prunes and some of the sauce. Pass rest of sauce separately.

Barbecued Pork
with Tropical Fruit Salsa

Serves 4 to 6.

2   **cloves garlic, minced or pressed**

½   **teaspoon dried oregano leaves**

¼   **teaspoon cumin seeds, coarsely crushed**

¼   **teaspoon crushed, dried, hot red chiles (optional)**

½   **cup lime juice**

½   **cup rum**

1½   **pounds compact-piece of boneless pork**

Tropical Fruit Salsa (recipe follows)

In a large zip-top plastic bag combine garlic, oregano, cumin seeds, chiles, lime juice and rum. Add pork, turning to coat. Seal bag and refrigerate 4 hours or until next day, turning bag over once or twice.

Remove pork from bag, reserving marinade. Barbecue about 25 to 30 minutes, basting with marinade. Slice thinly across grain to serve.

Tropical Fruit Salsa

Makes about 4 cups.

1   **medium-size ripe mango, peeled and cut in about ½-inch dice**

1   **cup fresh pineapple, diced**

½   **cup red bell pepper, diced**

⅓   **cup seasoned rice wine vinegar**

2   **tablespoons fresh mint, minced**

½   **teaspoon red pepper flakes, crushed (optional)**

2   **kiwis, peeled and cut into ¼-inch pieces**

In a medium size bowl mix mango, pineapple, bell pepper, vinegar, mint and red pepper. Cover and refrigerate for up to 2 days. Just before serving, add kiwi.

Spicy Cajun Pork Stew

Serves 6 to 8.

1	tablespoon vegetable oil
3	pounds boneless pork, cut into bite-size pieces

Salt and pepper

1	large onion, chopped
1	head garlic, all cloves chopped
2	14½-ounce cans ready cut tomatoes
1	teaspoon cayenne pepper
1	tablespoon paprika
½	teaspoon dried thyme
1	teaspoon dried basil
2	15-ounce cans red kidney beans

Rice

Heat oil in a large, heavy pot over high heat. Season pork with salt and pepper, and brown in 3 separate batches. Return all batches to pot and add onion and garlic. Cook 5 minutes. Add tomatoes with liquid, cayenne, paprika, thyme and basil. Cover pot, reduce heat to medium low and simmer for 1 hour until pork is tender. Drain beans and add to pork mixture. Taste to correct seasonings. Cook just until beans are heated. Serve over plain rice.

Baked Barbecue Spareribs

Makes enough sauce to serve 4 to 6.

¾   **cup molasses**

¾   **cup catsup**

¾   **cup onion, chopped**

1   **tablespoon grated orange rind**

⅔   **cup orange juice**

Dash Tabasco sauce

1½ **tablespoons Worcestershire sauce**

1½ **tablespoons olive oil**

2   **cloves garlic, minced**

1½ **tablespoons vinegar**

2-3 **whole cloves**

1   **teaspoon mustard**

¾   **pound lean pork ribs per person**

To make sauce combine molasses, catsup, chopped onion, grated orange rind, orange juice, Tabasco, Worcestershire sauce, olive oil, garlic, vinegar, cloves and mustard. Simmer 15 minutes. Simmer pork spareribs in lots of water for 15 minutes. Drain well. Place ribs flat in an ovenproof pan and cover with sauce. Bake at 350 degrees for 45 minutes.

Upside-Down Ham Loaf

Lean ground chicken or turkey can be substituted for ham and pork.

Serves 6 to 8.

1	**tablespoon butter**
½	**cup dark brown sugar**
1	**13-ounce can pineapple rings**
Milk	
1	**egg**
1	**cup soft bread crumbs**
2	**tablespoons mustard**
1	**teaspoon salt**
⅛	**teaspoon pepper**
1½	**pounds ground ham**
½	**pound ground pork**

Melt butter in an 8-inch x 8-inch loaf pan. Stir in brown sugar. Drain pineapple, reserving liquid. Arrange pineapple on brown sugar. Combine pineapple juice with milk to make 1 cup. Beat egg and stir in milk, bread crumbs, mustard, salt and pepper. Add ham and pork and mix well. Spoon meat mixture over pineapple. Bake at 350 degrees for 1 hour. Drain excess liquid. Invert onto platter.

Broiled Rosemary Chicken

Serves 4 to 6.

½	**teaspoon fresh rosemary, snipped**
	Pinch of dried thyme
½	**bunch green onions, sliced thin**
3	**tablespoons low-fat sour cream**
3	**tablespoons fresh lime juice**
2	**teaspoons Dijon mustard**
6	**chicken breast halves, skinned and boned**

Mix all ingredients except chicken breasts in a large 9 x 12-inch glass dish. Add chicken, turning to coat with marinade. Cover with plastic wrap and refrigerate overnight. Set oven to broil. Place chicken, heavily coated with marinade on broiler pan. Broil chicken 5 inches from heat for 5 minutes. Turn and broil about 5 minutes longer or until juices run clear.

Chicken Breast Parmesan

This is a pretty, no-fuss company dish.

Serves 4 to 6.

6	**chicken breast halves, skinned and boned**
⅔	**cup Parmesan or preferably Asiago cheese, grated**
3	**stalks celery, chopped**
3	**small tomatoes, chopped**
1	**teaspoon dry tarragon**
	Salt and pepper to taste
1-1½	**cups heavy cream**

Preheat oven to 350 degrees. Place chicken breasts in a large baking pan and sprinkle with half the cheese. Surround chicken with celery and tomatoes. Sprinkle with seasonings and pour cream over. Sprinkle with remaining cheese. Bake for 30 to 40 minutes. Add a salad, vegetable and pilaf for a lovely dinner.

Swiss Cheese Chicken

If you are looking for an attractive company dish, this is it!

Serves 8 to 12.

8	whole chicken breasts, boned, skinned and halved
2	tablespoons flour
1½	teaspoons salt, divided
1	teaspoon pepper
2	tablespoons butter
1	tablespoon oil
¼	cup dry sherry
1	teaspoon cornstarch
¾	cup half-and-half
⅓	cup dry white wine
1	tablespoon fresh lemon juice
½	cup grated Swiss cheese

Place chicken breasts in a bag with flour, 1 teaspoon salt and pepper. Close bag and shake the chicken to coat. Heat the butter and oil together in a 12-inch skillet. Brown chicken over moderate heat for 5 to 7 minutes per side. Add sherry, cover, and simmer over low heat until tender, about 20 minutes. Blend the cornstarch with half-and-half and remaining salt. Stir mixture into pan drippings and continue cooking until the sauce thickens slightly, about 5 minutes. Add the wine and lemon juice and heat a few minutes more. Sprinkle the cheese over the top of chicken. Cover the pan, remove from heat and let stand for 15 minutes. (The recipe may be made up to this point and held in the refrigerator for up to 24 hours. Reheat at 300 degrees.) Place the chicken under a preheated broiler to brown and glaze the top. Serve at once with rice or noodles.

Thai Curried Chicken and Potato

Serves 6 to 8.

1	tablespoon light soy sauce
1	tablespoon rice wine
2	teaspoons ginger juice
2	teaspoons cornstarch
2	pounds chicken breasts or thighs, boned and cut into 1-inch pieces
1½	tablespoons peanut oil
2	teaspoons garlic, minced
1	teaspoon fresh ginger, minced
2	tablespoons scallions, finely chopped
3	tablespoons Madras curry paste or powder, to taste
2	teaspoons salt
1	tablespoon sugar
2	cups coconut milk
2	tablespoons light soy
1	cup chicken stock
1½	pounds potatoes, peeled and cut into bite-sized pieces
	Fresh coriander for garnish

Make marinade of light soy, rice wine, ginger juice and cornstarch. Marinate chicken for 30 minutes. Heat wok or large skillet until hot. Add oil and quickly fry chicken for about 2 minutes. Add garlic, ginger and scallions and continue to stir-fry for 1 minute. Add curry, salt, sugar, coconut milk, soy and stock. Bring to a boil and pour contents into a clay pot or casserole. Cover and braise for 15 minutes. Add potatoes and braise for another 15 minutes or until potatoes are cooked. Skim surface fat. Garnish with coriander. Serve at once.

No-Time Lemon Chicken with Capers

This makes a very tasty leftover.

Serves 6.

4   **chicken thighs, skinned**

4   **chicken legs, skinned**

4   **chicken half-breasts, skinned**

Olive oil

¾   **cup dry white vermouth**

Salt and pepper

1   **4-ounce jar of capers**

3   **lemons, cut in wedges ½-inch thick at widest, skin side**

In a Dutch oven, brown chicken quickly in olive oil and add vermouth, salt, pepper, capers and seeded lemon wedges. Cover and cook at 350 degrees for 45 minutes to 1 hour. Serve with rice and salad. Two whole chickens can be cut up and substituted for chicken parts.

Indonesian Grilled Chicken
Serve with Lemon Pilaf with Currants and Almonds.

Serves 4.

2	**cloves garlic, minced**
½	**teaspoon salt, optional**
1	**teaspoon ground ginger**
1	**teaspoon ground coriander**
3	**tablespoons Ketjap Manis or Ketjap Benteng Manis**
3½	**tablespoons lemon juice**
¼	**cup water**
1	**pound chicken breasts, boned, skinned and cut into 1-inch cubes**

In a mortar with pestle, mash together the garlic, salt, ginger and coriander. Combine with Ketjap Manis, lemon juice and water. Place chicken and the marinade in a ceramic or glass bowl. Mix well. Marinate about 1 hour. Soak 8-inch bamboo skewers in water for about 15 minutes. Skewer chicken and broil about 5 or 6 inches from the heat until done, approximately 5 to 6 minutes on each side.

Ketjap Manis and Ketjap Benteng Manis are Indonesian soy sauces. If unavailable, you may substitute 1½ tablespoons regular soy sauce mixed with 1½ tablespoons molasses.

Plaza Vina Del Mar Park, in the center of Sausalito's downtown, was originally built in 1904 to provide a green space amidst the railroad tracks. William Faville, Sausalito resident and architect of much of the Panama-Pacific International Exposition, arranged to recast two great elephants from the Exposition and transport them here to guard the entrance of this charming park.

Mediterranean Chicken Kabobs

Serves 6.

24	**chicken tenders, about 1½ pounds (see note)**
¾	**cup white wine or apple juice**
¼	**cup chopped fresh parsley**
¼	**cup chicken broth**
1	**tablespoon fresh marjoram leaves**
2	**tablespoons low-fat mayonnaise**
2	**teaspoons honey**
½	**teaspoon salt**
¼	**teaspoon pepper**

Place chicken in shallow glass or plastic dish. Place remaining ingredients in blender. Cover and blend 30 seconds. Pour over chicken. Cover and refrigerate for 1 to 2 hours. Set oven to broil. Spray rack of broiler pan with nonstick cooking spray. Thread chicken on 12 10-inch skewers. Broil about 5 to 7 inches from heat for 3 minutes. Turn and spoon more marinade over chicken. Broil about 3 minutes longer or until chicken is done. Can also be barbecued. Serve with pilaf and vegetables.

Note: Boneless, skinless chicken breasts naturally separate into 2 pieces, the smaller of which is the "tender."

In 1941 Bundles for Britain, a Second World War volunteer effort, began to collect clothes for those in need. The current Sausalito Salvage Shop on Princess Street continues the tradition of volunteer collections for charity.

Garlic Chicken with Vegetables

Quick and easy for 2 people.

Serves 2.

2	tablespoons olive oil
4	chicken thighs, skinned and trimmed of fat
6	small new potatoes, cut in ½ or ¼'s
1	clove garlic, minced
1	teaspoon dried rosemary
⅓	cup chicken broth
2	carrots, sliced
	Salt and freshly ground pepper
¼	pound green beans, ends removed

Heat oil in a skillet and brown chicken thighs and potatoes. Reduce heat slightly when adding garlic so it does not burn. Add rosemary and toss. Add broth, carrots, salt and pepper. Cover and cook over low heat, stirring occasionally, adding broth if needed, until chicken and vegetables are done. Cook green beans separately and add just before serving.

Curried Baked Chicken

Serves 4.

4	**chicken breasts, skinned**
3	**tablespoons olive oil**
3	**tablespoons butter**
½	**cup onions, chopped**
½	**cup celery, chopped**
1	**clove garlic, minced**
1	**bay leaf**
1½	**cups apples, peeled and diced**
5	**tablespoons raisins, soaked in water to plump**
4	**tablespoons chutney**

Salt and freshly ground pepper

1½	**tablespoons curry powder**
1	**cup cream**

Shredded coconut

Preheat oven to 400 degrees. Brown chicken in butter and oil, and set aside. Add onion, celery, garlic and bay leaf and cook until soft, about 10 minutes. Add apples. Cook about 2 minutes more. Drain raisins and add to mixture. Add chutney. Remove from heat. Place chicken breasts in shallow baking dish. Do not stack or overlap. Season with salt and pepper. Spread apple mixture over chicken. Mix curry powder in cream and pour over chicken. Bake about 30 minutes, watching carefully and basting a couple of times. Remove from oven. Scatter coconut on top. Serve.

Easy Chicken Curry

Serves 4.

4	**boneless chicken breasts**
2	**tablespoons butter**
2	**tablespoons oil**
2-6	**teaspoons curry powder**
1½-2	**cups boiling chicken broth**
Salt and pepper	
4-6	**teaspoons cornstarch**
⅓	**cup cold water**

CONDIMENTS
Sliced green onions, coconut, peanuts, raisins, chopped hard boiled egg, and chutney

Cut chicken into pieces. Heat butter and oil in skillet, add curry powder and cook gently, stirring 2 to 3 minutes. Add chicken and coat with curry mixture. Add enough boiling broth barely to cover meat. Simmer for 8 to 10 minutes. Mix cornstarch with cold water, and add to curry. Cook, stirring 1 to 2 minutes until thickened. If too thick, thin with a little hot broth or water. Serve at once over hot steamed rice. Accompany with 4 or more condiments served in separate bowls. Leftover lamb can be substituted for chicken.

Chicken Respite

Serves 8 to 10.

1	head garlic, cloves peeled and minced
2	large onions, chopped
4-5	pounds chicken parts
2	teaspoons cumin
1	14-ounce can chicken broth
1	cup aged wine vinegar
2	15-ounce cans of diced tomatoes
2	tablespoons oregano
2	tablespoons rosemary
4	bay leaves
6	chopped carrots
3	stalks celery, sliced thin
10	mushrooms, quartered
¼	cup brandy
8-10	large potatoes, cooked and mashed
1	cup sour cream

Brown garlic and onion in large skillet until golden. Add chicken parts and cumin. When brown remove to Dutch oven or casserole. Add chicken broth and wine vinegar to skillet and reduce by half, removing all browned bits from bottom of pan. Pour into casserole. Add tomatoes, oregano, rosemary, bay leaves, carrots, celery, mushrooms and brandy. Cover and bake at 375 degrees for ½ hour. Prepare potatoes while cooking chicken and add sour cream to mashed potatoes. Spread potatoes over chicken mixture, covering evenly to edge of casserole. Use a fork to make a crisscross design in potato topping. Cook uncovered for 30 more minutes.

Wine-Smoked Game Hens

Quite a bit of work, but worth the effort!

Serves 4.

4	tablespoons olive oil
2	tablespoons fresh sage, minced, plus 4 sprigs
2	tablespoons fresh thyme, minced, plus 4 sprigs
1	tablespoon fresh parsley, minced

Salt and pepper to taste

4	Cornish game hens
1	green apple, cored and cut in 4ths
1	small onion, peeled and cut in 4ths
4	small cloves garlic, peeled
1	cup wood smoking chips (not mesquite)
½	cup water
½	cup red wine

In a small bowl mix olive oil, 2 tablespoons each of minced sage and thyme, parsley, salt and pepper. Rub birds inside and out with mixture. Place apple slice, onion slice, clove garlic, sprig of thyme and sprig of sage in each bird's cavity. Tie legs and wings of birds over breasts. Soak wood smoking chips in enough water and wine to cover for at least 30 minutes. Start fire in a barbecue chimney using newspaper or twigs, as the smell from lighter fluid will over-power the herbs and wood smoke. Mound lit coals on opposite side of fire grate and put drip pan down the middle. When coals are white hot, distribute ½ of wood chips on coals. Place birds down center of grill. Put lid on barbecue. After 30 minutes, add the rest of wood chips and more coals to the fire, if needed. Cook 30 minutes more with lid on. Check birds for doneness. Cook until juices run clear.

Confit of Duck with Roasted Yellow Finn Potatoes

You must begin this recipe 2 days before serving.

Serves 4.

1	**4- to 5-pound duck**
2	**tablespoons ground allspice**
5	**large cloves garlic, sliced**
1	**tablespoon fresh rosemary**
2	**tablespoons kosher salt**
1-1½	**pounds vegetable shortening**
4	**bay leaves**
1	**tablespoon black peppercorns**
Olive oil	
Salt and fresh ground pepper	
4	**yellow finn potatoes, 5-ounces each**
4	**large cloves of garlic, sliced**
1	**medium onion, quartered**
1	**tablespoon unsalted butter**

Day 1: Cut duck into quarters, 2 legs, 2 breasts, leaving some bones attached. Lay skin side down and sprinkle allspice, garlic, rosemary and salt over meat. Sandwich the 2 breasts and 2 legs together, skin side out, cover and refrigerate overnight.

Day 2: Melt shortening in heavy pot. Add bay leaves, peppercorns and duck quarters meat side down. Add more shortening, if needed, to cover duck. Simmer uncovered for about 3 hours on a low heat until tender. Never boil. Allow duck to cool in shortening for 2 hours. Remove duck, cover and refrigerate overnight. Duck is now ready for reheating and serving. (The shortening can be refrigerated and used again.

Day 3: Preheat oven to 400 degrees. Use 2 nonstick baking pans. Moisten 1 pan with reserved shortening and heat. Place duck pieces skin side down and put in oven. Moisten other pan with olive oil

Confit of Duck (continued)

and salt. Wash potatoes and cut lengthwise in quarters. Place in pan skin side up. Put potatoes in oven. After 10 minutes add garlic, onions and butter. Potatoes are done when tender and undersides are golden brown about 30 minutes. Duck is ready when skins are golden brown.

Wine-Basted Barbecued Turkey

Serves 6 to 8.

BASTING SAUCE

1	**cup white wine**
¼	**cup olive oil**
2	**tablespoons butter**
1	**onion, minced**
1	**clove garlic, crushed**
1	**teaspoon salt**
¼	**teaspoon paprika**
2	**teaspoons rosemary, minced**
1	**teaspoon parsley, minced**

Small turkey, turkey roll or ½ turkey

Simmer all ingredients for Basting Sauce for 15 minutes. A small turkey is good on the rotisserie. Turkey roll or ½ turkey can be roasted at 350 degrees or barbecued. Baste every 15 to 30 minutes until done.

Rolled Turkey Breast with Apple, Apricot and Currant Stuffing

Serves 10 to 12.

7	tablespoons chopped dried apricots
¼	cup currants
6	tablespoons unsalted butter, divided
½	medium onion, chopped
6	tablespoons slivered almonds
2	medium-size tart green apples, peeled, cored and diced
2¼	cups dry bread crumbs
½	teaspoon salt
¼	teaspoon dried sage, crumbled
3-4	tablespoons chicken stock
1	5- to 5½-pound fresh whole turkey breast, boned and trimmed
3	cups apple cider
½	cup applejack
1½	cups crème fraîche
	Additional applejack, optional
	Fresh lemon juice, optional
	Fresh sage

Soak apricots and currants in boiling water to cover until plumped and soft. Drain. Melt 1 tablespoon butter in heavy skillet over medium heat. Add onion and cook until slightly softened, about 6 minutes. Remove to a large bowl. Melt 1 tablespoon butter in same skillet. Add almonds and stir until golden brown, 2 to 3 minutes. Remove to a large bowl. Melt 2 tablespoons butter and add apples and cook until slightly softened, about 5 minutes. Remove to a bowl. Combine apricots, currants, onion, almonds, apples, bread crumbs, salt and sage. Blend in 3 tablespoons chicken stock. If stuffing is too dry, add 1 more tablespoon stock. Cool completely. Can be prepared 1 day ahead and refrigerated.

Rolled Turkey Breast (continued)

To butterfly turkey, lay meat skin side down. Starting at center, slice one side of breast in half almost to edge. Repeat on other side. Open meat where cut and spread out flat. Cover with waxed paper. Gently pound to thickness of ½ to ¾-inch. Season with salt. Spread with stuffing, leaving ½-inch border. Starting with long edge, roll meat into 16-inch x 3-inch cylinder. Tie at 1 to 2-inch intervals with twine and secure end with toothpicks.

Preheat oven to 350 degrees. Mix cider and applejack. Rub turkey with remaining 2 tablespoons butter. Set on rack in roasting pan. Roast until skin is brown and juices run clear, basting every 15 minutes with ½ cup cider mixture, about 1 hour. Let stand 15 minutes. Meanwhile degrease basting liquid left in pan. Pour into measuring cup and add enough remaining cider mixture to make 1½ cups liquid. Pour back into roasting pan and deglaze. Add crème fraîche and boil until sauce thickens. Strain sauce. Season with salt. If sauce is too sweet, add applejack and lemon juice to taste. Remove twine and tooth-picks and cut into ½ to ¾-inch slices. Arrange on platter. Garnish with sage. Pass sauce separately.

Roast Turkey with Rosemary and Pancetta

Serves 10 to 12.

1	**14-pound turkey**
	Olive oil
½	**pound pancetta ham, cut in small dice**
4	**sprigs rosemary**
2	**large cloves garlic, coarsely chopped**
	Salt and pepper
1	**teaspoon minced fresh thyme**
1	**teaspoon minced fresh sage leaves**
4	**tablespoons minced fresh rosemary**
2	**teaspoons minced garlic**
2	**cups dry white wine**

Rinse turkey inside and out and pat dry. Oil the cavity. Cut ¼ pound of pancetta into very small dice and the rest in larger chunks. Put the large chunks of pancetta, rosemary, garlic, salt and pepper into the cavity. Truss and tie well. Mix thyme, sage, rosemary, pancetta and garlic together. Slide some of the mixture all the way under the skin, getting it as far back as possible. Repeat with remainder of filling, massaging evenly. Spread a little olive oil on top of the skin and set the turkey in an oiled roasting pan. Bake at 350 degrees for 3 to 3¼ hours, basting with wine every 20 minutes. Slice and serve, being sure to include some of the fine pancetta, herb and garlic mixture on every plate.

Turkey Burgers
with Garlic Hot-Pepper Sauce

The sauce is not as hot as you might think!

Serves 4.

1	pound ground turkey
½	cup fresh bread crumbs
1	egg or equivalent substitute
2	tablespoons evaporated milk
¾	teaspoon salt
½	teaspoon freshly ground pepper
1	tablespoon vegetable oil
1	small onion, finely chopped
1	small clove garlic, minced
4	hamburger buns, grilled or toasted

GARLIC HOT-PEPPER SAUCE

¼	cup vegetable oil
¼	cup Dijon mustard
¼	cup minced garlic (about 10 cloves)
3	tablespoons red wine vinegar
1½	teaspoons crushed red pepper
½	teaspoon salt

Mix ground turkey with bread crumbs, egg, evaporated milk, salt and pepper. Cover and refrigerate. Light grill. Heat oil in a small skillet. Add the onion and cook over high heat until beginning to brown, 3 to 4 minutes. Stir in the garlic and remove from heat. Let cool, then stir into turkey mixture. Form the turkey into 4 patties. Cook on an oiled grill for about 6 minutes per side. In a glass or ceramic bowl combine all ingredients for Garlic Hot-Pepper Sauce. Serve turkey burgers on buns with sauce.

Baked Bass with Tomato Basil Sauce

*This sauce is also good warm on spaghetti
and cold on cold poached salmon.*

Serves 4 to 6.

3½-4   **pound piece of striped bass**
1   **onion, chopped**
1   **cup celery, chopped**
Salt and freshly ground black pepper
1   **tablespoon lemon juice**
2   **tablespoons olive oil**
2-3   **cloves garlic, minced**
4   **large shallots, finely chopped**
6   **tomatoes, peeled and chopped**
1   **cup fresh basil leaves, finely chopped**
3   **anchovies, finely chopped**
1   **tablespoon capers**
2   **tablespoons parsley, minced**
**Garnish of basil leaves, black olives, lemon
       and watercress**

Place bass on a large piece of heavy duty aluminum foil on a bed of chopped onion and celery. Season fish with salt and pepper, and sprinkle with lemon juice. Close foil tightly and place in baking pan. Bake at 350 degrees for 40 to 50 minutes. In a large skillet, heat the olive oil and sauté the garlic and shallots until soft and transparent. Add the tomatoes and basil, and cook until thick and all the juices have evaporated. Add anchovies, capers and parsley and just heat through.

To serve on platter, pour sauce around fish and garnish with basil leaves, black olives, lemon wedges and sprigs of watercress.

Halibut and Summer Vegetables in Parchment

Serves 4.

4	parchment sheets, cut into 8-inch hearts
4	teaspoons olive oil
4	red potatoes, blanched
½	red onion, thinly sliced
2	pounds fresh halibut
12	tomato slices
1	tablespoon fresh thyme, chopped
1	tablespoon red and yellow peppers, diced
2	tablespoons zucchini, diced
4	tablespoons fish stock
4	tablespoons white wine

Preheat oven to 325 degrees. Brush parchment with olive oil. Slice blanched potatoes ¼-inch thick. Dip sliced onion in boiling water to blanch. Set aside. On each piece of parchment, arrange slices of potato on one side of heart, followed by halibut, onions, tomato, thyme and diced vegetables. Spoon stock and wine over each one. Fold empty side of heart over the other. Beginning with the largest side, fold over and over along the perimeter of paper. Continue along all sides until the point of heart. Fold end over and tuck underneath. Bake for 10 to 12 minutes. Serve immediately.

Grilled Salmon with Red Pepper Sauce

An easy method for a most succulent fish.

Serves 6 to 12, depending on size of salmon.

1   **whole salmon, boned, butterflied with skin**
Juice of 2 lemons or limes
1   **bunch fresh dill, ½ chopped, remainder for garnish**
Pepper
2   **tablespoons olive oil or butter, if desired**
1   **bunch cilantro or parsley**

Light fire in covered barbecue. Place salmon on 2 layers of heavy-duty aluminum foil and crunch edges up around fish so that cooking juices can be caught, but entire top of fish is showing. Squeeze lemon juice over salmon, sprinkle on dill and lots of pepper. Add oil or butter. When coals are just ready, distribute along outside circle.

Put salmon on grate, cover barbecue and check in 20 minutes. If salmon needs more cooking, leave on 5 to 10 minutes only. Fish will continue to cook a little after removing it from fire. Serve from aluminum foil, but garnish with lots of dill, cilantro or parsley around edges. Serve with a corn or mango salsa, or a red pepper sauce.

Red Pepper Sauce

Makes 2 cups.

2   **roasted red peppers, chopped into ½-inch pieces**
1   **cup cream**
Salt and cayenne pepper

To roast peppers, place directly on gas flame (or under a hot broiler). Rotate with tongs until charred all over. Put in paper bag for about 5 minutes. Wash off blackened skin in cold water. Remove pith and seeds and cut in pieces. In saucepan combine peppers and cream. Boil until reduced by half, about 8 minutes. Purée in food processor. Season to taste.

Salmon with Horseradish Crust

Serves 4.

4	**salmon steaks or salmon fillets**
¼	**cup mayonnaise (low fat works well)**
2-3	**teaspoons of horseradish**
2	**teaspoons honey, heated so it is syrupy**
¼	**teaspoon dried tarragon**
¼	**teaspoon paprika**
Salt and pepper	

Preheat oven to 325 degrees and lightly grease baking dish to hold the salmon. Remove as many bones as possible and place the salmon in baking dish. Mix remaining ingredients and spread evenly over the salmon. Bake for 15 minutes. If desired, place the cooked salmon under the broiler for a few minutes to lightly brown the crust. Serve immediately.

Petrale Sole Roll-Ups

Very simple, but very good.

Serves 4.

2	**medium zucchini, grated**
¼	**cup plus 2 tablespoons shredded Parmesan cheese**
Salt and pepper	
4	**petrale sole fillets, about 1 pound total**

Mix together grated zucchini, ¼ cup Parmesan cheese, salt and pepper. You can sprinkle mixture with salt to taste, but try it without first because the cheese is salty. Spoon onto center of fillets and roll fillet around the mixture. Place in baking dish with overlapping ends down. Bake at 350 degrees for about 20 to 25 minutes. During the last 5 minutes sprinkle top of rolls with more shredded Parmesan cheese.

Phyllo-Wrapped Sole Fillets

Perfect every time!

Serves 6.

1	**cup cooked, flaked crabmeat**
½	**cup mushrooms, chopped**
1	**tablespoon fresh parsley, minced**
¼	**teaspoon dried dill weed**
½	**teaspoon salt**
¼	**teaspoon pepper**
1	**cup soft bread crumbs**
6	**fillets of sole**
12	**sheets of phyllo dough**
½	**cup butter, melted**

In a small bowl combine the crabmeat, mushrooms, parsley, dill, salt, pepper and bread crumbs. Spoon crab mixture onto centers of fillets of sole. Fold ends of fillets over filling, overlapping ends.

Keep phyllo sheets covered with a slightly damp cloth until needed to prevent drying. Brush melted butter on 1 phyllo sheet and top with a second phyllo sheet. Brush again with melted butter and fold buttered phyllo sheets in half. Place one stuffed fillet on center of prepared phyllo. Fold long sides of phyllo over top, slightly overlapping. Fold ends over fillet, slightly overlapping again. Place wrapped fillet, seam-side down on an ungreased 13-inch x 9-inch baking dish. Brush with butter. Repeat with remaining fillets. Bake at 375 degrees for 25 minutes, until phyllo pastry is golden.

Rolled Fillets with Bay Shrimp

*This can be turned into a great company dish by topping
with your favorite hollandaise or Mornay sauce.*

Serves 4.

6	tablespoons butter, divided
1	clove garlic, minced
1	onion, chopped fine
¼	cup green pepper, chopped fine
¾	pound bay shrimp
¼	cup day-old bread crumbs
1	tablespoon parsley, minced
¼	cup chives, chopped
2	teaspoons tarragon
½	teaspoon salt
⅛	teaspoon white pepper
4	fillets of sole or flounder

Melt 3 tablespoons of butter in skillet and sauté garlic, onions and green pepper. Remove from heat and add shrimp, bread crumbs, parsley, chives, tarragon, salt and pepper. On boned side of each fillet, spoon on filling mixture. Roll up fillet and tuck extra stuffing into ends. Melt 2 tablespoons butter in 6-inch x 10-inch baking dish. Arrange fillets in dish overlapped side down. Brush with 1 tablespoon melted butter. Bake at 350 degrees for 25 minutes.

Cioppino

A great fish stew that takes advantage of Sausalito's famous seafood catch.

Serves 8.

3	onions, chopped
3	bunches green onions, chopped
3	bell peppers, chopped
6	garlic cloves, minced
½	cup olive oil
¾	pound mushrooms, quartered
3	cups red wine
1	15-ounce can tomato sauce
2	1-pound, 12-ounce cans ready-cut tomatoes
1	chili pepper, seeded and minced, or 5 dashes Tabasco sauce
1	bay leaf
1½	teaspoons oregano
2	tablespoons chopped fresh basil
¼	cup fresh lemon juice

Salt and freshly ground pepper

2	dozen clams, well scrubbed
2	pounds red snapper, cut in 1½-inch pieces
3	dozen prawns, shelled
2-3	Dungeness crabs, cooked, cleaned and cracked

In a large soup kettle, sauté onions, peppers and garlic in oil for 5 minutes. Add mushrooms and sauté for 5 minutes more. Add wine, tomato sauce, tomatoes, chili, bay, oregano, and basil. Simmer, covered, for 1 hour.

About ½ hour before serving, bring sauce to a boil, lower to a simmer, add lemon juice, salt and pepper. Add clams and simmer 5 minutes. Add snapper and shrimp and simmer 3 more minutes, just until shrimps are pink. Add crab pieces to the pot (if you wish, you can remove crabmeat from the white body parts before adding to

Cioppino (continued)

the stew). As soon as the crab is heated through, check for seasonings and serve immediately in big soup bowls. All you need for a party is lots of sourdough bread, a big salad, a hearty red or white wine, and big napkins or bibs.

Sausalito Crab Cakes

Serves 6.

1	**pound cooked crabmeat**
¼	**cup celery, finely chopped**
¼	**cup green onions, finely chopped**
¾	**cup day old bread crumbs, divided**
1	**tablespoon mustard powder**
1	**tablespoon lemon juice**
1	**tablespoon Worcestershire sauce**
½	**teaspoon Tabasco sauce**
½	**teaspoon salt**
½	**teaspoon white pepper**
½	**cup mayonnaise**
1	**egg, beaten**
4	**tablespoons olive oil**

Pick through crabmeat to be sure all bits of shell are removed. Place in strainer to drain off excess liquid. Combine crabmeat, celery, onion, ¼ cup bread crumbs, mustard powder, lemon juice, Worcestershire sauce, Tabasco sauce, salt, pepper, mayonnaise and egg. Form mixture into 12 patties, approximately 2½-inches by ½-inch thick. Flatten patties and cover both sides with remaining ½ cup breadcrumbs. Keep refrigerated until ready to use. Heat oil in large skillet. Fry crab cakes for 2 minutes each side until golden brown.

Crabmeat and Artichoke Casserole

Serves 8 to 10.

3   **packages frozen artichoke hearts, cooked**
2   **pounds cooked crabmeat**
1½   **pounds mushrooms, sliced or quartered**
8   **tablespoons butter, divided**
6   **tablespoons flour**
3   **cups milk**
Dash cayenne pepper
2   **tablespoons Worcestershire sauce**
¾   **cup sherry**
1   **cup grated Parmesan cheese**
Paprika

Arrange artichokes in a layer in buttered, shallow baking dish. Pick through crab to make sure all bits of shell are removed. Spread layer of crabmeat over artichokes. Sauté mushrooms in 2 tablespoons butter for about 6 or 7 minutes and layer over crab. Make a medium cream sauce by melting 6 tablespoons butter in a saucepan and stirring in the flour, salt, pepper, cayenne pepper. Slowly add milk and cook until thickened. Add Worcestershire and sherry to white sauce and pour over top of casserole. Sprinkle with Parmesan cheese and paprika. Bake at 325 degrees for 45 minutes.

Greek Prawns

This is a close version of some delicious prawns
tasted in the seaside town of Piraeus outside Athens.

Serves 2.

¼   **cup unsalted butter**

2   **cloves garlic, minced**

¼   **cup dry white wine**

12-14 **medium uncooked prawns, shelled with tails left on**

1-2   **tomatoes, diced**

⅓   **cup feta cheese, coarsely crumbled**

1   **tablespoon cilantro, minced, optional**

In a large skillet, heat butter, garlic and wine over medium heat until butter melts. Turn up heat until mixture almost boils. Add prawns and tomatoes, stirring for 3 minutes, or until prawns are pink and firm. Remove from heat and stir in the feta. Serve over rice and sprinkle with cilantro.

Thai Prawns

Serves 4.

½   **cup coconut milk**
½   **teaspoon red pepper flakes**
3   **cloves garlic**
2   **fresh chili peppers, or Anaheim peppers**
½   **teaspoon coriander seed**
Zest of 1 lime
½   **bunch cilantro**
¼   **cup olive oil**
1   **1-inch piece gingerroot, peeled**
Juice of 1 lime
1½ **pounds large prawns, peeled and deveined**

Combine coconut milk, red pepper flakes, garlic, chili peppers, coriander seed, lime zest, cilantro, oil and gingerroot. Purée in blender. Marinate prawns in mixture 3 to 4 hours. Just before cooking, remove from marinade. Over high heat, boil marinade with lime juice until sauce is reduced by one-third. Add prawns and sauté until pink or done. Do not overcook prawns. Serve over rice or noodles.

Breads

Sausalito Houseboats

Dating from the 1880's when floating arks dotted the shallow waters of Richardson's Bay, Sausalito houseboats were first built as hunting and fishing clubs. Later, wealthy Victorian families who wanted to summer aboard on the bay built more elaborate floating homes.

As bridges replaced ferryboats around San Francisco Bay, many obsolete ferries were brought to rest beside abandoned steam schooners and old arks along Sausalito's waterfront. These were joined by salvaged World War II vessels, remnants of Marinship and its monumental war effort.

Rising out of these humble origins, many post-war houseboats were built by legendary bohemians, artists, writers and musicians, who were drawn to the area for its scenic beauty and its promise of an uncomplicated and unconventional lifestyle. Names like Sterling Hayden, Jean Varda, Alan Watts, Spike Africa, Lou Rawls, Juanita Musson, Shel Silverstein, and others became synonymous with the floating houseboat community that flourished here in the decades following the Second World War.

By Susan Frank

Pepper Biscuits

The trick to good biscuits is to have all your wet ingredients
very cold and to keep them cold. Do not be afraid to stop and
refrigerate the dough if it feels warm.

Makes 16.

1	chicken bouillon cube
1	tablespoon boiling water
2	cups flour
1½	teaspoons baking powder
2	teaspoons pepper, freshly ground
1	teaspoon salt
1	tablespoon minced chives
5	tablespoons cold butter, cut up
½	cup milk
1	egg

In a glass measuring cup, crush the bouillon cube, add boiling water and stir. Set aside to dissolve. Put flour, baking powder, pepper, salt and chives in a large mixing bowl. Stir to combine. Cut in butter with pastry cutter or 2 knives until mixture resembles coarse meal with lumps (just a few).

Add milk to measuring cup, stirring so bouillon mixes. Add egg and stir to combine thoroughly. Mixture should be ⅔ cup; if not, add or remove milk. Stir milk mixture into flour mixture. It will form a dough. Put this on pastry board and form into a ball. Flour board only if it needs it. Knead 12 to 15 times. (At this point you can freeze, refrigerate or cut dough.) Roll out dough to ½-inch thickness or thicker, and cut with a small glass or cookie cutter. Reroll scraps and cut. (This is another place to freeze, refrigerate or continue.) If possible, refrigerate biscuits on cookie sheet for 15 to 20 minutes before baking. They rise better. Bake 10 to 15 minutes at 400 degrees.

Corn-Cheese Muffins

Makes 6 large or 12 regular-size muffins.

- 1¼ **cups flour**
- 1 **cup yellow cornmeal**
- ⅓ **cup sugar**
- 3½ **teaspoons baking powder**
- 1 **cup firmly packed shredded cheddar cheese, about 4 ounces, divided**
- 1 **4-ounce can diced green chiles**
- 1 **cup milk**
- 1 **large egg**
- ¼ **cup butter or margarine, melted**

In a large bowl mix flour, cornmeal, sugar and baking powder. Reserve 2 tablespoons cheese. Stir remaining cheese and green chiles into flour mixture. Form a well. In a small bowl beat together milk, egg and butter. Pour liquid ingredients into flour well and stir until lightly blended. Spoon batter into muffin pan. Sprinkle reserved cheese over muffins. Bake in 400 degree oven for 20 minutes for regular-size muffins or 25 to 30 minutes for large muffins. Serve warm.

Puffed Cheese Ring

Similar to Yorkshire pudding, this bread turns
a bowl of soup or salad into a great lunch or light supper.

Makes 7 puffs.

1	**cup milk**
½	**cup butter**
½	**teaspoon salt**
	Dash cayenne pepper
1	**cup flour**
4	**eggs**
1	**cup shredded Swiss cheese, divided**

Put milk, butter, salt and cayenne in a 2-quart saucepan. Bring the mixture to a full boil, and over medium heat add the flour all at once. Cook and stir vigorously until mixture clings together and leaves the side of the pan, about 2 minutes. Remove the mixture from the heat, cool slightly, and beat in the eggs, 1 at a time, until the mixture is shiny, smooth and thoroughly blended. Stir ½ the cheese into the batter. Allow to cool.

Using about ¾ of the dough, make 7 equal mounds, arranged on a greased cookie sheet in a circle and touching each other. With the remaining dough make a small ball on top of each of the mounds Sprinkle the top with the remaining cheese. Bake in the middle of a preheated 375 degree oven for 45 to 55 minutes or until puffs are crisp and brown. Do not open the oven while ring is puffing or it will fall. Serve hot with butter.

Sourdough Bread

*The Bay Area's popular sourdough bread goes with almost any meal.
To make your starter, begin several days ahead. If you have a starter,
begin the night before baking the bread.*

Makes 2 loaves.

STARTER
- 1   package dry yeast
- 2   cups lukewarm water
- 2   cups flour

BREAD
- 1   cup starter
- 2   cups lukewarm water
- 6   cups flour
- 1   package dry yeast
- 1   tablespoon salt
- Cornmeal
- 1   egg yolk
- 1   tablespoon water

To make starter, dissolve yeast in water in large bowl. Add flour and mix well. Cover tightly with plastic wrap and let stand in cool place but do not refrigerate, for 2 days. Stir well before using. Starter may be stored in the refrigerator indefinitely, but must come to room temperature before use. To replenish starter after each use, stir in 1 cup water and 1 cup flour; cover and leave out overnight and then refrigerate. Keep replenishing indefinitely.

The night before making bread, remove 1 cup of starter from the bowl of starter stored in your refrigerator (replenish the starter bowl as indicated above and clearly mark this "starter bowl"). In a large bowl, combine the starter with 1 cup of lukewarm water and 2 cups of flour. Cover this large bowl with plastic wrap and let it sit in a cool place overnight. Next day, dissolve the yeast in remaining 1 cup of lukewarm water; let this stand five minutes, then add to sourdough mixture. Add salt and enough flour to make a soft dough. Knead about 10 minutes, adding more flour until smooth and elastic. Trans-

Sourdough Bread (continued)

fer to large greased bowl. Cover tightly with plastic wrap and let stand in warm place about 2 hours until doubled in volume. Punch down and transfer to floured board. Knead briefly and shape into 2 loaves. Place on baking sheet sprinkled with cornmeal. Let rise 1 hour in warm place, covered loosely with clean dish towel. Brush loaves with egg yolk mixed with water. Bake at 425 degrees for 25 minutes until it sounds hollow when tapped. Cool on rack.

Raisin Bread

Delicious toasted for breakfast ... and fat free.

Makes 1 loaf.

- **3   cups self-rising flour**
- **3   tablespoons sugar**
- **1   tablespoon cinnamon**
- **¾   cup walnuts, chopped**
- **1   cup raisins**
- **1   12-ounce can beer (not dark) at room temperature**

In a large bowl mix together flour, sugar and cinnamon. Add walnuts and raisins. Stir in the beer until batter is combined well. Spoon the batter into a well-buttered 9-inch x 5-inch loaf pan. Bake the bread at 350 degrees for 45 to 50 minutes, or until toothpick inserted in center comes out clean. Turn the bread out onto a rack and let it cool before slicing.

Adrianne's Honey Walnut Bread with Mock Devonshire Cream

Makes 1 loaf.

1	**cup milk**
1	**cup honey**
½	**cup sugar**
¼	**cup butter, softened**
2	**egg yolks**
2½	**cups sifted flour**
1	**teaspoon salt**
1	**teaspoon baking soda**
½	**cup walnuts, coarsely chopped**

Scald milk. Add honey and sugar. Stir over medium heat until sugar is dissolved. Cool mixture. Beat in butter and egg yolks. Sift flour with salt and baking soda. Stir into the batter and blend thoroughly. Fold in walnuts. Pour batter into a buttered and floured loaf pan. Bake at 325 degrees for about 1 hour or until toothpick inserted in center comes out clean. Leave the bread in the pan for 15 minutes, and then turn out on a wire rack to complete cooling. When cool cut into thin slices. Serve with Mock Devonshire Cream, sweet butter and honey, or with cream cheese and preserves.

Mock Devonshire Cream

8	**ounces soft cream cheese**
½	**cup thick sour cream**

Beat cream cheese with sour cream until the mixture is smooth and light, adding a little more sour cream, if necessary.

Sweet-Simit Braided Bread Twists

These are also great served with cheeses. Reduce the amount of sugar, if desired.

Makes about 48 twists.

1	**cup butter (can use ½ butter and ½ vegetable oil)**
1	**cup sugar**
4	**eggs**
¼	**cup milk**
1	**teaspoon vanilla**
5	**cups flour**
3	**teaspoons baking powder**

Pinch of salt

Sesame seeds

Soften butter to room temperature. Beat until light and fluffy. Add sugar, 3 of the eggs, milk and vanilla. Beat well to blend. Sift together flour, baking powder and salt. Combine with egg mixture. Knead until well blended. Pinch off an egg-sized piece of dough and roll with hands on a floured board until it is about 8 inches long and about the thickness of a pencil. Make a simple twist and place on a cookie sheet that has been sprayed with cooking oil or lined with parchment paper. Repeat with remaining dough. Beat the one remaining egg and brush twists to glaze. Sprinkle with sesame seeds. Bake at 350 degrees for 20 to 25 minutes or until golden brown. Twists keep for several weeks in an air tight container.

In 1946 a proposal to route Highway 101 along the Sausalito waterfront united the residents in protest. The SWC played a large role in fighting to defeat this potentially destructive plan, and the highway took its present course, west of town, over the Waldo Grade.

Aunt Mary's
Powdered Sugar Doughnuts

Makes about 2 dozen doughnuts and 3 dozen doughnut holes.

2   **tablespoons margarine**
1   **cup sugar**
1   **egg**
1   **cup milk**
4   **cups flour**
4   **teaspoons baking powder**
½   **teaspoon cinnamon**
1   **teaspoon salt**
    Vegetable shortening or oil for frying
    Powdered sugar

Cream margarine and sugar. Add well-beaten egg and milk. Sift flour with baking powder, cinnamon and salt, then add to wet ingredients. Add enough more flour to make dough stiff enough to roll. Work with ⅓ of dough at a time. On lightly floured board knead slightly to make smooth. Roll to about ¼ inch thick. Cut with floured doughnut cutter. Bring 2 to 4 inches of oil to 360 degrees (test with candy thermometer), and fry about 2 minutes on one side. Turn once and brown other side. Drain on paper towels. When partially cool, drop several doughnuts and doughnut holes at a time into a paper sack containing powdered sugar. Shake until well covered. Place on wire rack to cool completely. Best if served immediately.

Black Currant Muffins

These also make delicious mini-muffins for teas.

Makes 18 muffins.

2	**cups flour**
1	**tablespoon baking powder**
½	**teaspoon salt**
1	**cup sugar**
1	**egg, beaten**
⅓	**cup melted butter**
½	**cup sour cream**
½	**cup milk**
2	**teaspoons grated lemon peel**
1½	**cups dried currants**

STREUSEL TOPPING (OPTIONAL)

½	**cup flour**
¼	**cup brown sugar, packed**
¼	**cup butter**
¼	**teaspoon cinnamon**

Sift flour, baking powder, salt and sugar together. Stir in the egg, butter, sour cream and milk until just blended. Fold in lemon peel and currants. Fill muffin pans ¾ full. Combine ingredients for streusel topping until crumbly. Sprinkle over muffins. Bake at 400 degrees for 20 minutes. Serve warm.

Adopt-A-Park is a resident volunteer program to care for 18 charming parks in our small community.

Fresh Ginger Low-Fat Muffins

Makes about 16 regular muffins or 24 mini-muffins

1	**4 to 5-ounce piece unpeeled fresh ginger**
¾	**cup plus 3 tablespoons sugar, divided**
2	**tablespoons finely grated lemon zest**
2	**cups flour**
½	**teaspoon salt**
¾	**teaspoon baking soda**
½	**cup unsweetened applesauce**
2	**eggs or egg substitute**
1	**cup buttermilk**

Cut the unpeeled ginger into chunks and place in a food processor. Process until finely minced. You should have about ¼ cup. In a small saucepan combine the ginger and ¼ cup of the sugar and cook over medium heat a couple of minutes, stirring until the sugar melts and the mixture is hot. Set aside to cool until lukewarm. In a small bowl stir the lemon zest and 3 tablespoons sugar together. Let stand for a few minutes, then stir in the ginger mixture. Set aside.

In a medium bowl stir the flour, salt and baking soda together. In a large bowl combine the applesauce and the remaining ½ cup sugar. Add eggs and beat well. Add the buttermilk and mix until blended. Add dry ingredients and stir until just blended. Stir in the ginger-lemon mixture. Spoon into greased muffin pans, filling about ¾ full. Bake at 375 degrees for 12 to 15 minutes until a toothpick comes out clean. Cool for 1 minute, then remove from muffin pans.

Orange-Almond Muffins

Makes 12 regular-size muffins or 6 large muffins.

2¼	**cups flour**
½	**cup sugar**
2½	**teaspoons baking powder**
½	**teaspoon baking soda**
¼	**teaspoon salt**
1	**cup sliced almonds**
½	**cup milk**
½	**cup orange juice**
¼	**cup butter or margarine, melted**
1	**egg**
1	**teaspoon grated orange peel**

Powdered sugar

In a large bowl, mix flour, sugar, baking powder, baking soda and salt until blended. Stir in almonds. Form a well in center. In a small bowl combine milk, orange juice, butter, egg and orange peel. Beat to blend. Pour liquid mixture into well of flour mixture, mixing lightly to blend. Batter should be lumpy. Spoon mixture into greased muffin pans. Sprinkle lightly with powdered sugar. Bake at 400 degrees for 20 minutes for regular muffin pans, or 25 to 30 minutes for large muffin pans. Serve warm.

Spicy Bran Muffins

These moist, low-fat muffins are lively with spices.

Makes 12 regular-size or 6 large muffins.

- 1½ **cups stone ground whole wheat flour**
- ½ **cup miller's bran**
- ¾ **teaspoon baking soda**
- ¼ **teaspoon freshly grated nutmeg**
- ⅛ **teaspoon ground cinnamon**
- ⅛ **teaspoon coriander**
- ⅛ **teaspoon allspice**
- ⅛ **teaspoon mace**
- 2 **teaspoons grated orange rind**
- ½ **cup peeled, chopped apple**
- ¼ **cup raisins**
- ¼ **cup chopped walnuts**

Juice of ½ orange
- 1 **cup buttermilk**
- 1 **egg, lightly beaten**
- ¼ **cup molasses**
- 1 **tablespoon vegetable oil**

In a mixing bowl, combine the flour, bran, baking soda, nutmeg, cinnamon, coriander, allspice and mace. Stir in the orange rind, apple, raisins and walnuts. Combine the remaining ingredients. Add to the dry mixture and stir quickly until blended. Lightly grease muffin pans and dust with whole wheat flour. Fill muffin pans two-third's full. Bake at 350 degrees for 20 to 35 minutes.

Oatmeal Coffee Cake

Serves 6.

- **1 cup oatmeal**
- **1¼ cups boiling water**
- **¾ teaspoon salt, divided**
- **1¼ cups flour**
- **1 teaspoon soda**
- **1 teaspoon cinnamon**
- **1 teaspoon nutmeg**
- **¾ cup butter or margarine, melted, divided**
- **1 cup walnuts, coarsely chopped**
- **1 cup coconut**
- **1 cup brown sugar**
- **3 tablespoons milk**

Pour boiling water over oatmeal. Stir in ½ teaspoon of the salt, flour, soda, cinnamon, nutmeg and ½ cup of melted butter. Pour into lightly greased cake pan. For topping, mix together walnuts, coconut, ¼ cup of melted butter, brown sugar, milk and ¼ teaspoon salt. Sprinkle over cake batter. Bake at 325 degrees for 25 to 30 minutes, or until a toothpick inserted in center comes out clean.

Oven Puffed Pancake

A hot oven puffs this pancake to make a delicious
base for either sweet or savory fillings.

Serves 4.

2   **tablespoons butter**
½   **cup flour**
½   **cup milk**
2   **eggs**
1   **teaspoon vanilla**
Pinch of salt

Preheat oven to 450 degrees. Place butter in a 9-inch round metal cake pan. Place in oven until butter melts. Watch carefully to prevent burning. Mix flour, milk, eggs, vanilla and salt in a bowl. Beat well with hand egg beater. Pour mixture into hot pan. Bake for 18 minutes until browned and puffy. Cut into quarters to serve.

For a sweet offering, fill pancake with a mixture of several fruits and sprinkle powdered sugar on top. Or simply serve with hot maple syrup and melted butter. For a savory filling, try scrambled eggs and sausage, topped with a sprinkling of fresh herbs. It's also lovely as a base for your favorite chicken salad.

Lemon Scones

Makes 12 regular scones or 24 tea biscuits.

2½	cups flour
1½	teaspoons baking powder
½	teaspoon salt
1	tablespoon grated lemon peel
½	cup cold butter, cut up
¼-⅓	cup sugar
½	cup milk
1	egg

GLAZE

1	tablespoon lemon juice
2	tablespoons sugar

Put flour, baking powder (use only 1 teaspoon if you are making tea biscuits), salt and lemon peel in a large mixing bowl. Stir to combine. Cut in butter with pastry cutter or 2 knives; flour and butter mixture should resemble coarse meal. Gently mix in sugar. Combine milk and egg thoroughly. Stir milk mixture into flour mixture to form a ball. Place dough onto lightly floured pastry board. Knead 12 to 15 times. At this point you can freeze, refrigerate or cut dough.

To make regular scones, form into two 6-inch rounds, cutting each into 6 wedges. Remove to cookie sheet. Bake 10 to 15 minutes at 400 degrees until golden.

To make daintier tea biscuits, roll dough to ¼-½-inch thickness, and cut with a small glass or cookie cutter. Reroll scraps and cut. This is another place to freeze, refrigerate or continue. Refrigerate on cookie sheet for 15 to 20 minutes before baking. For Glaze, mix lemon juice and sugar, and brush lightly onto scones or biscuits. When baking, watch carefully to avoid burning glaze.

Orange Scones

Makes 14 scones.

1	**cup all-purpose flour**
¾	**cup cake flour**
2	**tablespoons sugar, divided**
2	**teaspoons baking powder**
1	**teaspoon kosher salt**
½	**cup unsalted butter, chilled**
1	**teaspoon minced orange zest**
½	**cup currants**
½	**cup heavy cream**
	Baking parchment

In a medium bowl, blend flour, 1 tablespoon sugar, baking powder and salt. Cut the butter into ½-inch cubes and toss with flour mixture, coating the cubes lightly. Turn mixture onto clean work surface. With a rolling pin, roll butter into long thin flakes. Keep butter covered with flour as you roll. Put flour and butter mixture back into bowl. Add orange zest and currants. Stir lightly until well blended. Add cream and mix until just blended. Form dough into ball and turn onto a lightly floured board. Knead dough gently until it begins to hold a shape. Do not overwork. It should be slightly crumbly. Roll dough ¾-inch thick. Cut with 2-inch round cutter. Arrange on a parchment-lined baking sheet. Sprinkle with remaining sugar. Chill for 15 minutes. Bake at 375 degrees for about 20 minutes. Cool on rack. Serve with unsalted butter and jam.

Desserts

The History of Richardson's Bay

In 1838 Captain William Antonio Richardson - mariner, rancher, and founder of San Francisco and Sausalito - acquired Rancho Saucelito, more than 17,000 acres that reached from the Golden Gate to the top of Mount Tamalpais.

In 1841 Captain Richardson became the first permanent non-Native-American resident of Sausalito, when he moved his family from San Francisco (then called Yerba Buena) to a small wooden house near Whalers' Springs in old town Sausalito. From this location it was easier to provision visiting ships with water, wood, and beef, all readily available at his Saucelito ranchero. His hacienda became a center of hospitality where he entertained commodores, naval officers of the English and Russian men-of-war, and captains from whaling and trading ships. With the discovery of gold in California in 1848 Captain Richardson's sailing and provisioning business flourished, supplying the growing population of San Francisco. He also ferried hundreds of gold seekers from San Francisco to the inland river towns of Sacramento and Stockton.

One hundred years later, the quiet town of Sausalito experienced an upheaval that permanently altered its waterfront. The federal government mandated that Bechtel Corporation find a West coast port site to build ships for the war effort. Bechtel chose Sausalito, and within less than a month of the decision work began to develop what is now called the Marinship. Three months after that, in June 1942, the first keel was laid, and the first liberty ship was christened the William A. Richardson. In three and a half years, 113 liberty ships, oil tankers, and army invasion barges were built and launched as well as numerous ships outfitted and repaired.

Today many of the original shipyard buildings continue to be used for artists' studios, marine businesses, start-up companies, recording studios and other small enterprises. The character of the Sausalito waterfront was shaped by its use during World War II. Today numerous sailboats are berthed along the waterfront, and many arrive from around the world to visit.

By Marty Kortebein

Fresh Fruit Tart

Serves 8 to 10.

2	cups flour
2	tablespoons chopped crystallized ginger
1	cup brown sugar
1	teaspoon vanilla
½	teaspoon salt
1	cup unsalted butter, cut in pieces

Fresh sliced peaches, nectarines, apples or cherries, etc.

½	cup whipping cream or half and half
6	ounces cream cheese
1	cup sugar
4	eggs
½	teaspoon cinnamon

Pinch allspice

Pinch nutmeg

½	teaspoon rum extract

Whipped cream

Preheat oven to 350 degrees. For pastry, mix flour, ginger, brown sugar, vanilla and salt in a food processor. Add pieces of butter one at a time, while processing, until ball of dough forms. Press into a well greased 11-inch tart pan. Bake 10 minutes until dough sets.

For filling, arrange sliced fruit or cherries decoratively in cooled shell. Blend cream, cream cheese and sugar in food processor. Add eggs one at a time. Add cinnamon, allspice, nutmeg and rum extract. Pour over fruit and bake 30 minutes or until knife inserted in center comes out clean. Serve warm or cold with softly whipped cream.

Betsy's Lemon Curd Tartlets

This is one of the easiest, most delicious tart doughs.
For special events use 1-inch molds and top with suggested fruits.
For dessert use any of the larger tart molds.

Makes about 2 to 3 dozen tartlets.

1	**cup butter, softened**
½	**cup sugar**
1	**egg**
1	**teaspoon vanilla**
2	**cups sifted all-purpose flour**

Blueberries, raspberries and/or strawberries

Lemon curd (purchased or prepared from following recipe)

Powdered sugar

Preheat oven to 325 degrees. Cream butter and sugar thoroughly. Beat in egg and vanilla. Stir in flour. Press dough with fingers into buttered tart molds. Bake on cookie sheet until delicately browned and set. Pastry shells will keep in a tightly covered container for a week, or they can be frozen. Fill each cooked pastry shell with lemon curd. Arrange berries on top and sprinkle with powdered sugar.

For variety fill pastry shells with almond custard filling or cream cheese filling. Use any fresh fruits, prettily arranged and brushed with an apricot glaze. To make apricot glaze, warm about 1 cup of apricot jam over medium low heat, strain out the chunks of fruit and brush the fresh fruit with the warm liquid.

Lemon Curd

Also wonderful with pound cake, scones, gingerbread, and much more.

½   **cup butter**
½   **cup fresh lemon juice**
3   **teaspoons freshly grated lemon rind**
1½   **cups sugar**
5   **eggs, well beaten**

Melt butter in heavy saucepan. Add lemon juice, rind and sugar. Cook, stirring until sugar is dissolved. Add eggs and cook, stirring constantly with a wooden spoon until thick, for about 25 minutes. Cool, cover, and store in refrigerator for several weeks.

French Apple Tarts

Serves 4.

¼   **pound puff pastry, ready-made or homemade**
1   **egg, mixed with 1 tablespoon water**
2   **Granny Smith apples**
1   **teaspoon sugar**
¼   **cup apple or apricot jelly, melted**

Roll the puff pastry into two 8-inch squares about ¼-inch thick. Cut a ¾-inch strip off each side of the 2 squares. Brush the edges of squares with egg and water mixture. Gently press the strips along each edge to form a raised border. Chill thoroughly. Preheat oven to 400 degrees. Peel and core apples, and slice thin. Use a fork to prick the bottom of the pastry shells. Arrange overlapping apple slices in rows on top of pastry shells. Sprinkle with sugar and bake for 15 to 20 minutes until edges of pastry are brown and sugar caramelizes. Remove from oven and brush with jelly. Serve warm.

Pumpkin Tartlets

Here is another recipe for a cookie-type pastry crust.

Makes about 48 bite-size tarts.

TART PASTRY

2¾	**cups sifted all-purpose flour**
1	**teaspoon baking powder**
½	**teaspoon salt**
¾	**cup butter, softened**
1	**cup sugar**
2	**eggs**
1	**teaspoon vanilla**

PUMPKIN FILLING

1	**15-ounce can pumpkin pie filling**
	Whipped cream

Sift flour, baking powder and salt into bowl and reserve. Put butter and sugar in large bowl of mixer and blend thoroughly. Add eggs and vanilla, and beat until light and fluffy. Add flour mixture and blend until smooth. Chill 1 hour until firm. Roll out a small amount of dough at a time on floured board to ⅛-inch thickness. Cut into 3-inch rounds with floured cutter. Place in greased 2½-inch diameter tart pans arranged on cookie sheets.

For filling, follow directions on pumpkin pie filling label. Pour pumpkin pie filling into uncooked tart shells. Bake at 475 degrees for 10 minutes. Reduce heat to 350 degrees and bake 10 minutes longer. Test for doneness by inserting knife in center of filling. If blade comes out clean, remove tarts from oven. Cool and remove from tart pans. Top with sweetened whipped cream.

Pine Nut Torte

An unusual, moist cake that is baked in a crust.

Serves 10 to 12.

CRUST

1	**cup flour**
2	**tablespoons sugar**
6	**tablespoons butter**
1	**egg**
¼	**cup seedless raspberry jam**

FILLING

1	**8-ounce can almond paste**
6	**eggs, separated**
¼	**cup sugar**
¼	**cup flour**
¾	**teaspoon baking powder**
¾	**cup pine nuts, toasted, divided**
	Sugar

For crust, in a small bowl, mix flour and sugar. Add butter and rub with fingers until mixture is reduced to fine crumbs. Stir in egg with a fork. Press dough into a ball. Roll out to generously fit a 10-inch cake pan with removable bottom. Fit dough into pan, making a 1-inch high rim. Spread jam over dough.

For filling, crumble almond paste in a bowl. Add egg yolks, sugar, flour and baking powder, beating until smoothly blended. Whip egg whites just until they hold short distinct peaks. Beat ½ into almond batter, then fold in remaining whites and a generous ½ cup nuts. Pour batter into crust and scatter remaining nuts over surface. Bake at 350 degrees for 35 minutes until center feels firm when lightly touched. Cool, remove pan rim and sprinkle with sugar. Freezes well. Can be served on a bed of raspberry coulis and topped with fresh berries and whipped cream.

Macadamia Nut Pie

Serves 8 to 10.

CRUST

- 2¼ **cups flour**
- ¼ **teaspoon salt**
- ¾ **cup chilled margarine**
- 5 **tablespoons water**

PIE FILLING

- ½ **cup butter**
- ¾ **cup sugar**
- 3 **eggs, slightly beaten**
- ¾ **cup dark corn syrup**
- ¼ **teaspoon salt**
- 1 **teaspoon vanilla**
- 1½ **cups macadamia nuts, finely chopped**
- **Whipped cream**

For crust, blend flour, salt and cold margarine until crumbly like cornmeal. Add water and form into a ball. Roll out between 2 sheets of wax paper. Place in 10-inch ceramic flan pan.

For filling, cream butter and sugar together. When light and lemon-colored add beaten eggs. Blend in dark corn syrup. Add salt, vanilla and nuts and mix well. Pour mixture into flan pan. Bake at 350 degrees for 35 to 40 minutes. Garnish with whipped cream.

Houseboats, ferries, barges and other floating objects evolved into an active waterfront community. Forbes' Island, a floating 700-ton "barge-island" with 15 rooms and palm trees, resided for many years in the waters just off Sausalito. It has since moved to San Francisco's Pier 39.

Sweet Potato Pie

Serves 6.

1	**cup sugar**
2	**eggs**
½	**cup butter**
2	**cups cooked sweet potato, mashed**
1	**teaspoon allspice**
¼	**teaspoon cinnamon**
1	**teaspoons vanilla**

Pinch of salt

¼	**cup evaporated milk**
1	**pie crust**

Using low speed on electric mixer, blend sugar, eggs, butter, sweet potato, allspice, cinnamon, vanilla, salt and evaporated milk in large mixing bowl. Pour into pie crust. Sprinkle a small amount of sugar on surface of pie to enhance browning of surface. Bake at 375 degrees for 30 to 45 minutes until set and brown.

Lemon Chiffon Cheesecake

Serves 12.

CRUST

2	cups graham cracker crumbs (6 ounces)
½	cup butter

FILLING

¼	cup cold water
2	envelopes unflavored gelatin
¼	cup sugar
5	egg yolks
⅓	cup milk, scalded
3	8-ounce packages cream cheese, room temperature
½	cup fresh lemon juice
¼	cup orange-flavored liqueur
2	drops vanilla
5	egg whites, room temperature
½	cup sugar
	Finely grated peel of 2 lemons

For crust, preheat oven to 350 degrees. Blend crumbs and melted butter in large bowl. Press into bottom of 10-inch springform pan. Bake until firm for about 12 to 15 minutes. Let cool.

For filling, pour cold water into cup and sprinkle with gelatin. Let stand until softened about 5 minutes. Heat gelatin and water over hot water until melted. Reserve. Combine sugar with egg yolks in top of double boiler and beat well with hand mixer. Set over simmering water. Gradually add hot milk, beating constantly until thick for about 5 minutes. Add gelatin and stir. Let cool to lukewarm. Beat cream cheese in large bowl until smooth. Beat in small amount of yolk mixture, then fold in remaining yolks. Fold in lemon juice, orange-flavored liqueur and vanilla. Beat egg whites in large bowl until soft peaks form. Gradually add ½ cup sugar, beating until stiff but not dry. Fold into cheese mixture. Turn filling into crust, smoothing top. Chill until firm for 6 hours or overnight.

Crème Brûlée

Serves 12.

12   egg yolks
1   cup sugar
1   tablespoon vanilla
Grated nutmeg to taste
3   cups heavy cream
3   cups half-and-half
Brown sugar

Mix together egg yolks, sugar, vanilla and nutmeg. Scald the cream and half-and-half. Pour a little of the hot milk mixture into egg yolk mixture, stirring with a wire wisk and pour this mixture into the remaining milk in the pan. Pour into dessert cups (ramekins) in a pan of hot water. Bake at 225 degrees for 1 hour and 20 minutes, or until firm. Refrigerate. Just before serving crumble brown sugar over custard. Mist with water and brown quickly under broiler, watching carefully.

Summer Pudding

Serves 6.

1   quart summer fruits (apples, berries, black currants, plums, etc.)
½   cup sugar, or to taste
12-16 slices of stale white bread, crusts trimmed
Whipped cream

Stew fruit with sugar. Puree fruit a little. Soak bread slices in juice of stewed fruit. Line a china bowl or soufflé dish with bread slices. Put in ½ the fruit. Cover with a layer of bread. Add remaining fruit and top with another layer of bread. Put a plate on top and add a weight to press the pudding down. Refrigerate overnight. Turn out pudding onto serving plate and serve with whipped cream or thickened fruit juice, or both.

If properly made there should be no trace of white bread. For a sweeter dessert substitute pound cake for bread.

Hot Curried Fruit

Serves 12.

1	14½-ounce can peaches, drained
1	14½-ounce can Bing cherries, drained
1	14½-ounce can pineapple chunks, drained
2	11-ounce cans mandarin oranges, drained
4	pitted prunes, halved
12	dried apricot halves
2	bananas, cut in ¾-inch slices
⅔	cup brown sugar
2	teaspoons curry powder (or see variations)

Juice of 1 lemon
¼   **cup butter**

Butter an 8-inch x 12-inch casserole. Mix together all fruit and put into casserole. Mix together brown sugar and curry powder. Sprinkle over fruit. Squeeze lemon juice over all and dot with butter. Cover and bake at 300 degrees for 1 hour. For a variety substitute orange-flavored liqueur for curry. Or try cinnamon and nutmeg. Serve plain or with whipped cream or ice cream.

The Marin Fruit Company founder, Willie Yee, is remembered by the small waterfront park~Yee Tock Chee Park~ at the foot of Princess Street. In his neighborhood grocery, which closed in 1998, Willie was known for his care and concern, while serving residents of Sausalito for almost 70 years.

Upside-Down Cranberry Pudding

Serves 8.

½ **cup butter, divided**

1½ **cups fresh cranberries**

⅓ **cup sugar**

½ **cup chopped walnuts**

½ **cup sugar**

1 **egg**

½ **cup flour**

Whipped cream or ice cream

Preheat oven to 325 degrees. Melt 2 tablespoons butter in 9- or 10-inch pie pan. Spread cranberries, ⅓ cup sugar and walnuts evenly in pie pan. In mixing bowl beat egg with ½ cup sugar until thick. Beating constantly, add flour. Beat in remaining melted and cooled butter. Pour batter evenly over cranberries and nuts. Bake for 30 to 40 minutes or until browned. Cool, then run a thin knife around the pan sides to loosen. Invert until pudding slides out. Serve with whipped cream or ice cream.

Bread Pudding with Brandy Sauce

Serves 8.

4	**eggs**
1	**cup sugar**
1	**teaspoon vanilla**
½	**teaspoon salt**
½	**teaspoon nutmeg**
1½	**teaspoons cinnamon**
⅓	**cup butter, melted**
¾	**cup raisins**
¾	**cup chopped pecans, toasted**
3	**cups whole milk**
	14-16 ounces stale French or Italian bread, cubed

Beat eggs until frothy. Add sugar, vanilla, salt, nutmeg, cinnamon, melted butter. Beat until blended. Add raisins, pecans and milk. Pour over bread cubes. Push down bread into liquid and soak for 1 hour. Bake at 350 degrees for about 1 hour until puffed and firm in the center. Serve with Brandy Sauce.

Brandy Sauce

3	**eggs, separated**
1	**cup sugar**
3	**tablespoons butter, softened**
1	**cup whipping cream**
¼	**cup brandy**

Beat egg yolks, sugar and butter until well mixed and thick. Beat egg whites until stiff and fold into mixture. Whip cream, add brandy and fold into mixture.

If you are uncomfortable with uncooked egg, this recipe is not for you.

Lemon-Angel Dessert Cake

Serves 10.

6	**eggs, separated**
1½	**cups sugar, divided**
¾	**cup lemon juice**
1½	**tablespoons grated lemon rind**
1	**envelope gelatin**
¼	**cup water**
1	**small angel food cake**
1	**cup whipping cream**

Cook egg yolks, ¾ cup sugar, lemon juice and lemon rind in double boiler over simmering water, stirring constantly until thick. Soak gelatin in water. Add gelatin to yolk mixture and stir until melted.

Beat egg whites until soft peaks form. Beat in ¾ cup sugar until egg whites stand in peaks. Fold into lemon custard. Tear angel food cake into 1½- to 2-inch chunks. Alternately layer cake and custard in 10-inch tube pan until cake and custard is used, ending with custard. Refrigerate until set. Invert pan onto platter. Frost with whipped cream.

A number of SWC members have been elected to City Councils as well as many other commissions in town. Five have served as Mayor. While not a club member, Sally Stanford was elected on her fifth campaign in 1970. Her restaurant, the Valhalla, added to the color of Sausalito.

Fresh Peach Soup

Make this the day before you plan to serve it.

Serves 4 to 6.

5   **large ripe peaches, peeled and quartered**
¼   **cup sugar**
1   **cup plain yogurt**
¼   **cup fresh orange juice**
¼   **cup fresh lemon juice**
¼   **cup cream sherry**
Fresh mint for garnish

Puree peaches and sugar in food processor or blender. Blend in yogurt and add juices and sherry. Mix until smooth. Refrigerate overnight. Garnish with mint to serve.

Strawberry Sauce

This sauce has a wonderful fresh taste and
is delicious with angel food cake and vanilla ice cream.

Makes 2 cups.

3   **pints strawberries**
1   **tablespoon fresh lemon juice**
⅓   **cup orange-flavored liqueur**
½   **cup sugar**

In a large saucepan combine all the ingredients. Cook over low heat, stirring often, until sugar is dissolved and the sauce begins to thicken slightly, about 20 minutes. Put into food processor and process until almost smooth.

For variety try other combinations of fresh fruits and liqueurs.

Marty's Persimmon Pudding

Serves 6 to 8.

½	**cup butter**
1	**cup sugar**
1	**cup sifted flour**
¼	**teaspoon salt**
1	**teaspoon cinnamon**
2	**teaspoons baking soda**
2	**tablespoons hot water**
1	**cup persimmon pulp**
2	**tablespoons brandy**
1	**teaspoon vanilla**
1	**cup raisins**
½	**cup or more walnuts**

Melt butter and add sugar. Then add flour with salt and cinnamon. Dissolve soda in hot water. Add persimmon pulp, soda, brandy, vanilla, raisins and walnuts to flour mixture. Place mixture in greased molds such as 14½-ounce cans, filling them ¾ full; place molds in water bath with water halfway up side of molds. Cover molds loosely with aluminum foil and steam in 350 degree oven until fully cooked, about 2½ hours. Scoop pudding out of mold and serve with Rum Sauce.

Rum Sauce

2	**tablespoons butter or margarine**
1	**tablespoon flour**
2	**tablespoons sugar**
1	**cup milk**
2	**tablespoons rum or brandy**

Melt butter and stir in flour and sugar. Add milk and bring to a boil. Add rum or brandy.

Noel's Hazelnut Meringues with Lemon Filling

These were served at a Founders' Day Luncheon and High Jinks to rave reviews!

Serves 6 to 8.

MERINGUES

1	cup hazelnuts (about 5 oz.), toasted, husked
1¼	cups sugar, divided
3	tablespoons cornstarch
6	large egg whites, room temperature
1	teaspoon cream of tartar
¼	teaspoon salt
1	teaspoon vanilla extract

LEMON FILLING

3	cups sugar
⅔	cup cornstarch
3	cups water
6	egg yolks, slightly beaten
6	tablespoons butter
½	cup lemon juice
2	tablespoons grated lemon rind
	Whipped cream

For meringues, preheat oven to 225 degrees. Line 2 large baking sheets with baking parchment. Finely grind hazelnuts, ¼ cup sugar, and cornstarch in food processor. Using electric mixer, beat egg whites, cream of tartar and salt in large bowl until thick and foamy. Gradually add remaining 1 cup of sugar, beating until whites are very thick and glossy peaks form. Fold hazelnut mixture and vanilla into meringue. Form nests for individual desserts on parchment paper. Bake until firm and just beginning to color but not hard, about 1 hour and 10 minutes. Turn off oven, close door and let meringues dry overnight. Carefully peel parchment off meringues.

Noel's Hazelnut Meringues (continued)

For lemon filling, mix sugar and cornstarch in saucepan. Gradually stir in water. Cook over medium heat, stirring constantly, until mixture thickens and boils. Simmer 1 minute. Slowly stir egg yolks into hot mixture. Simmer 1 minute longer, stirring constantly until smooth. Remove from heat and blend in butter, lemon juice and lemon rind. Let cool slightly. Spoon into center of meringues. Serve with whipped cream.

Raspberry Trifle

An easy version of a classic.
You can substitute a variety of fruits for the raspberries.

Serves 12.

1   **3-ounce package regular vanilla pudding mix**
2   **cups of milk**
1   **8-ounce container whipped cream substitute**
1   **pound cake**
1   **10-ounce jar raspberry jam**
2   **12-ounce packages frozen raspberries with juice**
¼-½ **cup rum, brandy, sherry or favorite fruit liqueur**

Prepare vanilla pudding using milk according to directions. Cool completely. Then combine with whipped cream substitute. Slice pound cake into ¼-inch slices. Spread one side only with jam and place jam-side down on bottom and around sides of clear glass bowl. Sprinkle rum on the pound cake. Spread some of the frozen raspberries and juice on the pound cake. Spread a layer of pudding mixture on top of the fruit and pound cake. Continue to layer the ingredients starting with pound cake jam-side down, finishing with the pudding mixture on top. Make several hours ahead, even a day ahead, so that flavors blend. Refrigerate until 30 minutes or so before serving.

Scottish Trifle

An elegant, classic trifle recipe.
You will need a pretty glass dish of 2 quart capacity.

6	**whole eggs, divided**
½	**teaspoon vanilla**
¾	**cup sugar plus 1½ tablespoons sugar**
½	**cup flour**
1½	**cups milk**
¾	**cup cream**
6	**egg yolks**
⅔	**cup sugar**
1	**teaspoon vanilla**
2	**tablespoons cornstarch**
1	**cup raspberry preserves**
1	**29-ounce can pears**
1	**cup whipping cream**
2	**tablespoons powdered sugar**
1	**teaspoon vanilla**

Preheat oven to 425 degrees. Line a 12 x 16-inch jelly-roll pan with parchment paper and set aside. To make sponge cake roll, put 3 whole eggs, 3 egg yolks and vanilla into mixing bowl and beat with electric beater while gradually adding ¾ cup sugar. Beat until thick and creamy, about 4 minutes. Fold flour into mixture, about ⅓ amount at a time. In a separate bowl, beat to soft peaks, 3 egg whites, add 1½ tablespoons sugar and continue beating until stiff. Carefully fold beaten whites into egg yolk mixture and pour into prepared jelly-roll pan, spreading with a spatula and bake 10 minutes until lightly browned. Remove from oven and turn out onto sheet of parchment paper.

To make crème anglaise, heat milk and cream. In a mixing bowl beat together 6 egg yolks, ⅔ cup sugar, 1 teaspoon vanilla. Stir cornstarch into mixture with a wire whisk. Pour a little of the hot milk mixture into egg yolk mixture, stirring with a wire whisk and pour this mixture into the remaining milk in the pan. Cook gently until the custard thickens.

Scottish Trifle (continued)

To assemble the trifle, cut jelly roll into ¼-inch slices, spread each slice with a little raspberry preserve and arrange a layer in the serving dish. Next arrange a layer of sliced pears on top. Continue with a second layer of jelly roll slices and a second layer of pear slices. Pour on crème anglaise, cover and chill in the refrigerator. Before serving, beat whipping cream, powdered sugar and 1 teaspoon vanilla and pipe onto the trifle using a pastry bag fitted with an open star tip. Can place fresh raspberries on top.

Grand Marnier Sauce
Wonderful with fresh fruit.

Makes about 3 cups.

4	**egg yolks**
1	**teaspoon cornstarch**
½	**cup sugar**
1	**cup warm milk**
2	**tablespoons Triple Sec liqueur**
¼	**cup Grand Marnier liqueur**
1	**teaspoon vanilla**
1	**teaspoon grated orange rind**
1	**cup whipping cream, whipped**

In the top of double boiler, beat egg yolks, cornstarch and sugar until pale yellow. Add warm milk and blend. Set over simmering water. Stir constantly with wire whisk until mixture thickens and coats a spoon heavily. Remove from heat.

Stir in liqueurs, vanilla and orange rind. Let cool, then refrigerate for 2 to 3 hours. Just before serving fold whipped cream into the sauce. Another tablespoon of Triple Sec may be added if desired. Sprinkle more Triple Sec over fresh fruits, if desired.

World's Easiest Apple Cake

Serves 15.

4	**cups chopped, unpeeled, apples**
2	**eggs, well-beaten**
½	**cup vegetable oil**
2	**cups sugar (can be half white, half brown)**
1½	**cups raisins**
1	**cup chopped nuts**
2	**cups flour**
2	**teaspoons cinnamon**
2	**teaspoons baking soda**
1	**teaspoon salt**

Mix all ingredients together. Spread in greased 9-inch x 13-inch pan. Bake at 350 degrees for 50 to 60 minutes. Cool. Cut into squares and sprinkle with powdered sugar, or frost with Cream Cheese Frosting.

Cream Cheese Frosting

3	**ounces cream cheese, softened**
½	**cup butter, softened**
1	**cup powdered sugar**

Mix all ingredients thoroughly, and spread on cake.

Barbara's Spicy Beer Cake

An exceptionally tasty cake! Don't worry, beer never tasted so good.

Serves 10 to 12.

3	**cups flour**
2	**teaspoons baking soda**
1	**teaspoon cinnamon**
½	**teaspoon allspice**
½	**teaspoon ground cloves**
2	**cups chopped dates**
1	**cup chopped walnuts**
1	**cup butter**
2	**cups dark brown sugar**
2	**eggs**
2	**cups beer**

Mix flour, baking soda and spices. In a separate bowl, combine dates and walnuts, adding a small amount of flour to coat. Set aside. In a large bowl, cream together the butter and brown sugar. Add eggs one at a time, beating well after each addition. Add flour mixture alternately with beer. Mix well after each addition. Stir in dates and nuts. Pour into a greased and floured 12-cup fluted tube pan. Bake at 350 degrees for 1 hour and 15 minutes, or until toothpick comes out clean. Cool in pan on rack 10 minutes. Then turn out on rack to finish cooling. Serve with your favorite hard sauce, ice cream, or enjoy plain. This cake freezes well.

> *The Sausalito Woman's Club, a favorite spot for club activities, is often rented for wedding receptions, art shows and musical soirées.*

Carrot Ring Cake
A treasured family heirloom recipe.

Serves 8.

1	cup margarine or butter
1	cup brown sugar
2	eggs
2½	cups flour
¾	teaspoon baking powder
1	teaspoon baking soda
1	teaspoon salt
2	tablespoons water
2	tablespoons lemon juice
3	cups grated carrots, loosely packed in measuring cup

Preheat oven to 350 degrees. Cream margarine well. Add sugar and beat 1 minute with an electric mixer. Add eggs and beat for 3 minutes. Add sifted dry ingredients alternately with combined water and lemon juice. Stir in grated carrots. Spoon into greased and floured 6-cup ring mold. Bake for 45 minutes or until firm to the touch.

Let carrot ring cool for at least 30 minutes before inverting onto a serving plate. It may be served while slightly warm or at room temperature.

For a more heart-healthy cake use only ½ cup of margarine and it still tastes great.

Chocolate Sheet Cake

This cake has been baked for more events in Sausalito than any other.

Serves 20.

2	**cups flour**
2	**cups sugar**
1	**cup butter**
1	**cup water**
¼	**cup cocoa**
½	**cup buttermilk**
2	**beaten eggs**
1	**teaspoon vanilla**
1	**teaspoon soda**
1	**teaspoon cinnamon**

TOPPING

½	**cup butter**
¼	**cup cocoa**
6	**tablespoons milk**
1	**16-ounce box powdered sugar**
1	**teaspoon vanilla**
1	**cup chopped walnuts**

For cake, mix together flour and sugar in bowl. In a saucepan bring butter, water and cocoa to a boil. Then pour over flour and sugar mixture, and mix well. Add buttermilk, eggs, vanilla, soda and cinnamon, and mix well. Pour into a greased 10-inch x 15-inch jelly-roll pan. Bake at 400 degrees for 20 minutes until just done.

For topping, 5 minutes before cake is done, cook butter, cocoa and milk together. Bring to boil, then add powdered sugar, vanilla and walnuts. Spread over cake as soon as you take it from oven. It must be topped when cake is hot.

Orange Cake

Serves 12.

1   **large orange**

1   **cup raisins**

⅓   **cup walnuts**

2   **cups sifted flour**

1   **teaspoon baking soda**

1   **teaspoon salt**

1   **cup sugar**

½   **cup vegetable oil**

1   **cup milk**

2   **eggs**

TOPPING

⅓   **cup orange juice**

⅓   **cup sugar**

1   **teaspoon cinnamon**

For cake, cut orange into walnut-size pieces including rind and pulp (no seeds). Grind orange, raisins, and walnuts in a food processor. Sift the dry ingredients together in a bowl. Add the oil, milk and eggs and beat for 2 to 3 minutes until well blended. Mix in the orange mixture. Pour into a greased Bundt pan. Bake at 350 degrees for 45 to 50 minutes. Let rest 5 minutes. For topping, blend with a small wire whisk orange juice, sugar and cinnamon. Pour over the warm cake and allow cake to absorb juice. Unmold on a plate to serve.

Almond Macaroons

No fat, no cholesterol and only 30 calories each.

Makes 2½ dozen.

8   ounces almond paste
1   cup sugar
3   egg whites

Cut or break almond paste into very small pieces and put in blender or food processor. Add sugar and egg whites. Blend until smooth and lump free. Cover cookie sheet with greased wax paper, parchment paper or greased brown paper. Drop mixture onto paper by teaspoonfuls in mounds about the size of a walnut. Allow to dry at room temperature at least 2 hours before baking. Bake at 300 degrees for 30 minutes. Wet a towel and spread on kitchen counter. Lift paper with cookies still on it from cookie sheet and set on wet towel to cool. Let stand a few minutes until each cookie can easily be removed to wire rack.

Lace Cookies

An old Dutch recipe. For crisp, lacy cookies,
avoid baking them on a humid day.

Makes 4 dozen.

½   cup butter
1   cup brown sugar
1   cup flour
¾   teaspoon cinnamon
1   cup blanched almonds, finely chopped
¼   cup warm water

Cream butter and sugar. Sift flour with cinnamon and add to creamed mixture. Stir in almonds, then water. Drop by teaspoonfuls onto an ungreased cookie sheet. Bake in a preheated 325 to 350 degree oven for 10 minutes. Let cool 2 minutes. Then remove to wire rack to finish cooling.

For variety, substitute flaked coconut for nuts and add 1 teaspoon vanilla.

Chocolate Chip Applesauce Cookies

Makes about 5 dozen cookies.

4	**cups flour**
2	**teaspoons baking soda**
½	**teaspoon salt**
2	**teaspoons cinnamon**
1	**teaspoon nutmeg**
1	**teaspoon cloves**
1	**cup margarine or shortening**
2	**cups sugar**
4	**eggs**
2	**cups applesauce**
1	**cup raisins**
1	**12-ounce package chocolate chips**
½	**cup chopped walnuts**
2	**cups oatmeal**

Sift together flour, soda, salt, cinnamon, nutmeg and cloves into a bowl. In another bowl cream together margarine, sugar and eggs. Add applesauce and flour mixture alternately to creamed mixture. Add raisins, chocolate chips, nuts and oatmeal. Drop by teaspoonfuls onto cookie sheet. Bake at 350 degrees for 15 minutes.

Double Chocolate Oatmeal Cookies

Makes 5½ dozen smallish cookies.

1½	**cups sugar**
1	**cup butter, softened**
1	**egg**
¼	**cup water**
2	**teaspoons vanilla**
1¼	**cups flour**
⅓	**cup cocoa**
½	**teaspoon baking soda**
½	**teaspoon salt**
3	**cups regular oatmeal**
2	**12-ounce packages chocolate chips**

Cream together sugar and butter until fluffy. Add egg, water and vanilla. Add dry ingredients and mix until just blended. Add the chocolate chips. Dough is very stiff. Drop by teaspoonfuls onto a greased cookie sheet and bake at 350 degrees for 10 to 12 minutes. Bake longer for larger cookies, just until center is set. Do not let them brown around edges. Remove from cookie sheet immediately to cool.

Thankfully, current SWC prospective members are no longer screened by surprise committee visits to check for household cleanliness, one of many hurdles to membership in the old days.

Cranberry Drops

Makes about 4 dozen cookies.

½	cup butter
1	cup sugar
¾	cup packed brown sugar
¼	cup milk
2	tablespoons orange juice
1	egg
3	cups flour
1	teaspoon baking powder
½	teaspoon salt
¼	teaspoon baking soda
1	cup chopped nuts
2½	cups whole cranberries

Cream butter and sugars together. Beat in milk, orange juice and egg. Sift together flour, baking powder, salt and baking soda. Blend into sugar mixture. Stir in nuts and cranberries. Drop onto greased baking sheet by teaspoonfuls or spread in greased jelly-roll pan. Bake in 375 degree oven. Bake cookies for 10 to 15 minutes. If done in jelly-roll pan, bake for 20 minutes and cut into bars.

Sausalito community taste buds enjoy holiday favorites at the SWC Holiday Open House, usually on the first Sunday in December from 3-5 P.M. If you are in the area, stop by for the festivities.

Persimmon Cookies

Makes 4 dozen.

3	**large ripe persimmons**
½	**cup brown sugar**
½	**cup granulated sugar**
½	**cup butter or margarine**
1	**egg**
2	**cups flour**
1	**teaspoon baking soda**
1	**teaspoon cinnamon**
½	**teaspoon nutmeg**
1	**teaspoon vanilla**
½	**cup golden raisins**
½	**cup chopped walnuts or pecans**

Scoop pulp from persimmons to make 1 cup. Cream sugars and margarine until light and fluffy. Beat in egg. Add persimmon pulp, flour, baking soda, cinnamon, nutmeg and vanilla, beating until well blended. Stir in raisins and nuts. Drop by teaspoonfuls onto ungreased cookie sheet. Bake in preheated 350 degree oven for 12 to 14 minutes. Cool on rack.

Marzipan Bars

Makes about 24 cookies.

CRUST
½	cup butter
½	cup brown sugar
1	teaspoon vanilla
¼	teaspoon salt
1½	cups flour
¾	cup raspberry jam

FILLING
½	pound almond paste
½	cup sugar
1	teaspoon vanilla
3	large eggs

FROSTING
2	tablespoons butter, softened
1½	cups powdered sugar
2	tablespoons milk
1	teaspoon vanilla
1	ounce semisweet chocolate, melted

To make crust, cream together the butter, brown sugar, vanilla and salt. Beat in flour until mixture just forms a dough (can be done in food processor). Press the dough into the bottom of a 13- x 9-inch baking pan. Spread evenly with jam.

For the filling, cream together almond paste and sugar until smooth. Beat in vanilla and eggs, 1 at a time, until blended. Spread the filling over the jam. Bake the crust and filling in a 350 degree oven for 20 to 25 minutes until filling is pale golden. Cool.

To make frosting, beat together butter, sugar, milk and vanilla until mixture is smooth and beat in chocolate. Spread frosting over filling. Chill covered for 1 hour. Cut into bars.

Half-Way Cookies

Makes about 50 bar cookies.

1	cup butter
½	cup granulated sugar
½	cup brown sugar
2	egg yolks, slightly beaten
1	tablespoon water
1	teaspoon vanilla
2	cups sifted flour
¼	teaspoon salt
¼	teaspoon baking soda
1	teaspoon baking powder
1	6-ounce package chocolate chips

MERINGUE

2	egg whites
1	cup brown sugar

Cream butter and sugars. Add egg yolks, water and vanilla. Mix until smooth. Sift flour, salt, baking soda and baking powder together. Mix into creamed mixture. Makes a stiff dough. Pat out on a greased 14- x 10-inch jelly-roll pan. Sprinkle chocolate bits evenly over the dough.

For topping beat egg whites stiff and gradually add the brown sugar. Spread on top of the chocolate. Bake at 350 degrees for 20 to 25 minutes. Cool before cutting.

Turtles

Makes 2 dozen bar cookies.

CRUST
2	**cups flour**
1	**cup brown sugar**
½	**cup butter**

CARAMEL LAYER
⅔	**cup butter**
½	**cup brown sugar**
1	**cup pecans, coarsely chopped**
1	**cup chocolate chips**

Mix crust ingredients until particles are fine. Pat firmly in ungreased 12- x 9- x 2-inch pan.

Combine in saucepan butter and brown sugar. Heat until surface begins to boil. Remove from heat. Sprinkle pecans evenly over unbaked crust. Pour caramel layer over pecans. Bake at 350 degrees for 18 to 22 minutes, or until buttery and crust is golden brown. Immediately sprinkle with 1 cup of chocolate chips. Swirl chips as they melt. Leave some whole for a marbled effect. Cool and refrigerate so chocolate hardens before cutting into bars.

Snickerdoodles

Where in the world did this name come from?

Makes about 5 dozen cookies.

1	**cup butter, softened**
1½	**cups sugar**
2	**eggs**
2⅔	**cups sifted flour**
2	**teaspoons cream of tartar**
1	**teaspoon baking soda**
¼	**teaspoon salt**
½	**cup sugar**
2	**tablespoons cinnamon**

Preheat oven to 400 degrees. Mix butter and sugar thoroughly. Add eggs and mix thoroughly. Sift together flour, cream of tartar, baking soda and salt, and add to creamed mixture. Roll into balls the size of small walnuts. Roll in mixture of sugar and cinnamon. Place 2 inches apart on ungreased baking sheet. Bake for 8 to 10 minutes, until very slightly browned, but still soft. They puff up first, then flatten out. Cool.

For variety at Christmas roll in red or green sugar.

Biscotti

Twice-baked cookies to go with your coffee-yum!

Makes 2 dozen cookies.

½	**cup sliced almonds**
2	**eggs**
2	**egg whites**
1	**cup sugar**
2	**tablespoons unsalted butter, softened**
2	**tablespoons vegetable oil**
¼	**cup applesauce**
1	**teaspoon vanilla**
2	**teaspoons almond extract or orange-flavored liqueur**
2	**cups flour**
1	**teaspoon baking powder**
½	**teaspoon salt**

OPTIONAL INGREDIENTS

12	**ounces mini semisweet chocolate morsels**
3	**tablespoons unsweetened cocoa**
8	**ounces bittersweet or semisweet chocolate**

Preheat oven to 350 degrees. Spread almond slices on a cookie sheet and toast in oven for 5 minutes. Remove from oven and let cool.

Mix eggs, egg whites, sugar, butter, oil, applesauce, vanilla and almond extract in an electric mixer. In a separate bowl combine the flour with baking powder and salt. Add flour mixture and almonds to the egg mixture and combine thoroughly. If you want to do variation 1 or 2 as described below, add the appropriate ingredients now.

Divide batter in ½ and form 2 long "logs" of dough on a greased or parchment-lined cookie sheet. Leave space between the logs to give them room to expand. Bake for 25 minutes or until slightly golden. Let cool on cookie sheet for 10 minutes. Then while still warm, using a serrated knife, slice logs into even ½-inch slices. Rearrange slices, on their sides on the cookie sheet and toast in the oven for 12

Biscotti (continued)

minutes. Remove from oven and let cool completely. Variation 3 can be done now.

Variations

1. Mix in mini-semisweet chocolate morsels.

2. Mix ⅓ of dough with 3 tablespoons unsweetened cocoa. Then make cocoa dough mixture into 2 long noodles. Make 2 plain dough logs out of the remaining dough. Then take each plain dough log and wrap it around a cocoa noodle to create a cocoa-centered log. Place on the cookie sheet.

3. After making and cooking the basic recipe, coat 1 side of each cookie with chocolate as follows. Melt 8 ounces of bittersweet or semisweet chocolate in the top of double boiler. Line a cookie sheet with baking parchment. Pour the melted chocolate on the parchment paper and spread evenly. Quickly press cookies into the chocolate, laying cookies down as close as possible. Put the filled cookie sheet in the refrigerator for about 1 hour or until chocolate hardens. Remove cookies carefully so chocolate adheres.

Almond Ginger Shortbread

Makes 2 dozen cookies.

2	**cups unbleached flour**
1	**cup brown sugar**
1	**tablespoon ground ginger or to taste**
½	**cup ground almonds**
1	**cup butter**

Thoroughly combine all ingredients in food processor. Press into fluted-edged 10-inch cake pan, metal or ceramic, with or without removable base. Bake at 350 degrees for 1 hour. Cool 10 minutes in pan. Carefully mark out narrow wedges with a knife. When shortbread has cooled, cut through marks completely. Dust with powdered sugar before serving.

Mocha Pecan Balls

Makes about 5 to 6 dozen.

1	**cup unsalted butter, softened**
½	**cup granulated sugar**
2	**teaspoons vanilla**
1	**tablespoon instant espresso powder**
¼	**cup unsweetened cocoa powder**
¾	**teaspoon salt**
1¾	**cups flour**
2	**cups pecans, finely chopped**
Powdered sugar	

In a bowl cream butter with sugar until the mixture is light and fluffy. Add the vanilla, espresso powder, cocoa powder and salt. Beat until combined well. Add flour and beat until it is just combined. Stir in the pecans. Chill the dough, covered, for at least 2 hours or overnight.

Preheat oven to 375 degrees. Roll dough into 1-inch balls and arrange balls about 1-inch apart on baking sheet. Bake the cookies in batches for about 12 or 15 minutes until they are just firm. Let cool for 5 minutes. Toss warm cookies in batches in a bowl of powdered sugar to coat them well.

Fruit-Filled Cookies

These are like fruit newtons - but better.

Makes 4 dozen cookies.

FILLING
1	pound pitted prunes or dried apricots, chopped
½	cup brown sugar
¾	cup water
1	tablespoon lemon juice

PASTRY
½	cup butter or margarine
1	cup sugar
2	eggs
1	teaspoon grated lemon peel
1	teaspoon vanilla
1	tablespoon milk
2	cups flour
1	teaspoon baking powder
½	teaspoon salt
¼	cup chopped almonds or walnuts

Mix dried fruit, brown sugar and water. Cook, stirring, for about 10 minutes. Add lemon juice. Let cool.

Cream together butter and sugar. Beat in eggs, lemon peel, vanilla and milk. Sift flour, baking powder and salt into creamed mixture and mix well. Chill 3 hours or until firm. Roll out half of dough on a floured pastry cloth into a 12-inch square. Cut into 3 strips. Spread ⅓ cup filling down center of each strip. Top with 2 teaspoons of the nuts. Bring edges to center and seal. Turn seam down on greased cookie sheet. Cut in 1½-inch bars, leaving in place. Repeat with rest of dough. Bake at 375 degrees for 12 to 15 minutes.

Mama's Butter Cookies

Makes 6 dozen cookies.

1	**pound sweet butter**
1	**cup sugar**
¼	**cup whiskey**
4	**eggs, separated**
4	**cups flour**
¼	**cup powdered sugar**
¼	**cup granulated sugar**

Cream butter and sugar. Add whiskey. Separate eggs, and add yolks and blend thoroughly. Stir in flour.

On lightly floured surface roll dough to ¼-inch thickness. Cut with cookie cutter. Place on greased baking sheet. Beat egg whites until soft peaks form. Spread top of cookies with egg whites. Bake at 350 degrees for 12 to 15 minutes. Remove to rack and sprinkle with mixture of powdered sugar and granulated sugar mixture.

Apricot Balls

Wonderful, fruity dessert-great served with ice cream or sherbet.

Makes 50 small balls.

1	**pound dried apricots, chopped**
½	**cup golden raisins**
½	**cup whipping cream**
½	**cup almond-flavored liqueur**
2	**cups shredded coconut**
½	**cup finely slivered almonds**
½	**cup gingersnap crumbs**
	Powdered sugar

Mix apricots and raisins in a bowl. Sprinkle cream and liqueur over them and let stand overnight. Add coconut, almonds and gingersnap crumbs and blend well. Roll into small balls. Roll balls in powdered sugar. Chill and store in covered container in refrigerator.

Candied Walnuts

Excellent on their own, with fruit and cheese or in a salad.

Makes 4 cups.

2	**cups sugar**
2	**teaspoons cinnamon**
1½	**teaspoons salt**
10	**tablespoons water**
1	**teaspoon vanilla**
4	**cups walnuts**

Bring sugar, cinnamon, salt and water to a boil, cooking until soft-ball stage (240 degrees on a candy thermometer). Remove from heat and beat in vanilla. Add nuts. Stir to coat completely. Spread on foil and let cool. Store in an airtight container.

English Toffee

Made in the microwave.

Makes about 4 dozen squares.

1	**cup butter**
1	**cup dark brown sugar**
2	**1.55-ounce milk chocolate bars**
1	**cup chopped pecans, toasted**

Using a 4-cup glass measuring cup, microwave butter to melt about 2 minutes on high. Remove from microwave, add sugar and stir. Microwave 5 to 7 minutes on high, stirring once half way through cooking time (after about 2 minutes and 30 seconds). Cook until mixture is dark caramel in color, but not burnt.

Pour immediately in a 9 x 13-inch glass baking dish lined with aluminum foil that has been sprayed with oil. When firm in about 5 minutes, pour or siphon off the liquid, golden, clarified butter. Break chocolate in small pieces over top of caramel mixture and spread around until all chocolate is melted. Sprinkle nuts over all. When toffee is almost firm, cut into about 1½-inch squares. Remove toffee to airtight container when completely firm, in about 3 hours.

This and That

Sausalito Woman's Club Founders' Day Tradition

In February, as the air quickens with the promise of spring, unusual activities take place at the SWC clubhouse. Voices rise in song, feet move to measured steps, and laughter rings throughout the building. It's the Jinks show in rehearsal. This rite of passage for new members requires that they take an active role in the show. For some it's a chance to show talent they already have; for others it's their first bewildering debut on stage. For all, it's a time of closeness and of shared triumphs.

The Jinks is part of Founders' Day, a tradition that dates back to the 1920's when members of the club gathered at a luncheon to honor its founders. Simple skits have since blossomed into full-fledged productions with original scripts, music and choreographed dancing. Add costumes, scenery, lighting and a month of rehearsals by new and old members alike, and you are talking about a major effort.

The show and the luncheon itself remain a mystery to the club members until that day in March when they gather to honor the founders and presidents. The club auditorium is festooned with images reflecting the Jinks theme. From the chandeliers down to the programs on decorated tables, color and imagination reign.

All this for one day? Well, this is the High Jinks. On the following Saturday night a repeat performance, the Low Jinks, permits family members and guests of the cast to attend. That's it, and the show's cast, which at times has grumbled about the lengthy rehearsals, now wonders if the show could go on, on tour maybe? Many have found new skills and new friends. And that's what the Jinks and Founders' Day are all about.

By Hope McCrum

Muesli

Makes about 7 cups.

- **3**   **cups quick-cooking oatmeal, uncooked**
- **1**   **cup oat bran**
- **2**   **cups Grape Nuts cereal**
- **½**   **cup raisins**
- **¼**   **cup slivered almonds, toasted**

Combine all ingredients in a large container with a lid. When ready to serve, scoop out cereal and add milk, sugar, fresh fruit and yogurt, as desired.

You may add or substitute any other chopped dried fruits or nuts to this basic cereal recipe. Dried apricots are especially good. Ground flax seed is another healthy addition.

Honey Barbecue Sauce

Makes about 2 cups.

- **¾**   **cup honey**
- **1**   **6-ounce can tomato paste**
- **1½**   **teaspoons salt**
- **½**   **teaspoon pepper**
- **2**   **teaspoons ground ginger**
- **2**   **tablespoons concentrated frozen orange juice**
- **2**   **large cloves garlic, pressed**
- **2**   **tablespoons chopped onion**
- **2**   **tablespoons Worcestershire sauce**
- **3**   **tablespoons chopped parsley**

Mix ingredients in blender for 30 seconds. Apply lavishly to ribs, chicken, or whatever you wish.

Tim's Barbecue Sauce

This recipe was developed by the husband of one of our members.

Makes about 8 cups.

1	**12-fluid ounce bottle beer**
2	**14-ounce bottles catsup**
1	**12-ounce bottle chili sauce**
⅓	**cup yellow mustard**
1	**tablespoon dry mustard**
1½	**cups brown sugar**
2	**tablespoons ground black pepper**
1	**cup wine vinegar**
1	**cup lemon juice**
½	**cup steak sauce**
¼	**cup Worcestershire sauce**
2	**tablespoons soy sauce**
¼	**cup olive oil**
2	**tablespoons Tabasco sauce**
1	**head garlic, peeled and minced**

Combine all ingredients until well mixed. Refrigerate at least 3 days before using. Then enjoy.

Each year Sausalito celebrates the holidays with the lighted yacht parade. Boats of all kinds are festooned with lights and sail along the waterfront, one festive night in December.

Green Salsa

Makes about 2½ cups.

1	green bell pepper, seeded and cut into chunks
2	cups fresh or canned tomatillos, diced
¼	cup chopped onion
½	cup fresh cilantro leaves
3	jalapeño peppers, seeded
3	garlic cloves, crushed
1	tablespoon fresh lime juice
¼	teaspoon salt

Put all ingredients into blender or food processor and process until coarsely chopped.

Real Curry Powder

This easy recipe is best if made fresh each time.

Makes 3 to 4 tablespoons.

2	teaspoons coriander seeds
1	teaspoon cumin seeds
½	teaspoon yellow mustard seeds
1	teaspoon fenugreek
4	red dried chiles
2	teaspoons peppercorns
10	curry leaves
½	teaspoon dried ginger
1	teaspoon turmeric

Grind coriander seeds, cumin seeds, mustard seeds and fenugreek in spice grinder or coffee grinder until powdered. Add chiles, peppercorns, curry leaves, ginger and turmeric. Grind together until thoroughly powdered.

Red Pepper Relish with Aromatics

This recipe was given to us by Jerry Di Vecchio of Sunset Magazine,
*who served it as part of a Thanksgiving menu she prepared for us.
It's delicious any time of year, with a variety of meats and fish.*

Makes about 1½ cups.

1-1¼	**pounds red bell peppers**
1	**lemon**
1	**cup water**
1	**cup rice vinegar**
1	**cup sugar**

AROMATIC SPICE MIX

1	**tablespoon mustard seed**
1	**teaspoon coriander seed**
¼	**teaspoon fennel seed**
⅛	**teaspoon hulled cardamom seed**
⅛	**teaspoon ground nutmeg**
3-4	**whole cloves**

Stem, seed and thinly slice peppers. Trim ends from lemon and discard. Thinly slice lemon and cut slices into quarters; discard seeds. In a 4 to 5-quart pan combine peppers, lemon, water, vinegar, sugar and Aromatic Spice Mix ingredients. Bring to a boil over high heat and boil rapidly, stirring often, until liquid is almost evaporated, about 20 minutes. Take care not to scorch. Serve warm or cold. Stir before serving.

Can be made up to 1 week ahead, covered and refrigerated.

Pineapple-Peach Chutney

A wonderful condiment to serve with meat.

Makes about 4 cups.

1	**1-pound 13-ounce can sliced peaches**
1	**13½-ounce can pineapple chunks**
1	**cup dark raisins**
1	**cup light raisins**
1	**cup brown sugar**
2	**teaspoons salt**
⅓	**cup butter**
1	**teaspoon ground ginger**
1	**teaspoon dry mint**
½	**teaspoon chili powder**
½	**teaspoon cinnamon**
½	**teaspoon ground coriander**
Pinch saffron	
6	**whole cloves**
4	**whole cardamom, crushed**
1	**cup water**
2	**tablespoons white wine vinegar**
½	**teaspoon rose water**

Combine peaches and pineapple with their syrup in a large, heavy saucepan. Add all remaining ingredients except vinegar and rose water. Simmer 1 hour. Stir in vinegar and rose water. Cool. Turn into well-sealed jars and refrigerate.

> *"Settle in Sausalito; Live Long and Be Happy....."*
> *Sausalito News, first issue, February 12, 1885.*

Tomato-Raisin Chutney

Good with roasted lamb or chicken.

Makes about 4 cups.

3	**medium tomatoes**
½	**pound light raisins**
2	**tablespoons butter**
½	**cup water**
1	**teaspoon dry mint**
¼	**teaspoon ground mace**
¼	**teaspoon black pepper**
5	**whole cloves**
½	**teaspoon cinnamon**
1	**teaspoon salt**
½	**cup sugar**
2	**tablespoons white wine vinegar**

Scald and peel tomatoes. Cut into chunks. Rinse raisins and sauté in butter 2 minutes. Add tomatoes. Cook on medium heat for 7 minutes, stirring constantly. Place in the top of a double boiler over hot water. Combine water, mint, mace, pepper, cloves, cinnamon, and salt. Add to tomato mixture. Simmer uncovered for 1 hour. Add sugar and vinegar and cook 10 minutes longer. Chill well before serving.

The Army Corps of Engineers built a working model of the entire San Francisco bay and delta area in one of the large Second World War Marinship buildings. The model helps engineers and scientists study the tidal action and water flow of the bay. The Bay Model and its accompanying displays are open for visitors to wander through and enjoy.

Hot Horseradish Mustard

Good with beef, ham and sausages.

Makes about 1½ cups.

- ½   **cup dry mustard**
- ¼   **cup mustard seed**
- ½   **cup cider vinegar**
- ⅓   **cup white wine vinegar**
- 3   **tablespoons honey**
- 2   **tablespoons drained prepared horseradish**
- 1   **teaspoon red pepper flakes**

Combine all ingredients in blender or food processor until smooth. Store in tightly covered jars in refrigerator up to several months.

Old German Mustard Pickles

Makes 7 pints.

- ½   **cup prepared mustard**
- 4   **cups white vinegar**
- ½   **cup salt**
- 3⅓   **cups sugar**
- 3   **pounds whole pickling cucumbers**

Combine mustard, vinegar, salt and sugar. Bring to a boil. Add cucumbers and bring back to a full boil. Pour into hot, sterilized jars, filling to ¼-inch from top. Vinegar solution should cover pickles. Seal each jar immediately.

Remington's Dog Biscuits

This is a favorite dog treat at Sausalito's Remington Dog Park. Special bone-shaped cutters can be purchased at specialty pet stores.

Makes 80 4-inch biscuits.

4½	cups whole wheat flour
3	cups all-purpose flour
3	cups cornmeal
1½	cups oats
⅔	cup nonfat dry milk
2	tablespoons garlic powder
2	teaspoons salt
3½	cups beef broth
1	cup vegetable oil
2	large eggs

GLAZE

1	large egg
1	tablespoon Worcestershire sauce

Preheat oven to 300 degrees. Mix dry ingredients in large bowl. Mix broth, oil and 2 eggs in medium-size bowl. Stir broth mixture into flour mixture until blended and dough becomes soft. On a floured surface roll out dough to a ½-inch thickness. Cut to desired shape. Place ½-inch apart on ungreased cookie sheet. Mix egg and Worcestershire for glaze. Brush over top and sides of biscuits. Bake on two cookie sheets at a time for 2 hours. Turn off oven and leave in for another 2 hours to dry and harden. May be stored at room temperature for up to 3 months, or frozen.

Metric Conversions

Mass Weight

1 ounce (oz)	=	28 grams (g)
1 pound (lb)	=	450 grams (g)
1 gram (g)	=	.035 ounces (oz)
1 kilogram (kg) or 1000 g	=	2.2 pounds (lbs)

Liquid Volume

1 fluid ounce (fl oz)	=	30 milliliters (ml)
1 fluid cup (c)	=	240 milliliters (ml)
1 pint (pt)	=	470 milliliters (ml)
1 quart (qt)	=	950 milliliters (ml)
1 gallon (gal)	=	3.8 liters (l)
1 teaspoon (tsp)	=	5 milliliters (ml)
1 tablespoon (tbsp)	=	15 milliliters (ml)
1 milliliter (ml)	=	.03 fluid ounces (fl oz)
1 liter (l) or 1000 ml	=	2.1 fluid pints or 1.06 fluid quarts
1 liter (l)	=	.26 gallons (gal)

Metric Temperature Conversion

Fahrenheit	Celsius
150 degrees F	66 degrees C
200 degrees F	95 degrees C
250 degrees F	120 degrees C
300 degrees F	150 degrees C
350 degrees F	175 degrees C
375 degrees F	190 degrees C
400 degrees F	205 degrees C
450 degrees F	230 degrees C
475 degrees F	245 degrees C
500 degrees F	260 degrees C

Oven Temperature Chart

Slow	250 to 325 degrees F	120 to 163 degrees C
Moderate	325 to 400 degrees F	163 to 205 degrees C
Hot	400 to 450 degrees F	205 to 230 degrees C
Very hot	450 degrees F and above	230 degrees C and above

Equivalent Amounts

almonds	⅘ lb. unshelled	1 cup chopped
apples	1 lb.	3 cups sliced
apricots	1 lb.	6 cups cooked
beans, dried	½ lb.	1 cup
cheese, grated	4 oz.	1 cup
cheese, cream	3 oz.	6 tbsp.
chocolate morsels	6 oz.	1 cup
crumbs, graham	14 squares	1 cup
crumbs, saltines	28 squares	1 cup
crumbs, fresh bread	2 slices	1 cup
egg whites	8 to 10	1 cup
egg yolks	14 to 16	1 cup
flour	1 oz.	4 tbsp.
flour, all-purpose	1 lb.	4 cups sifted
flour, cake	1 lb.	4½ cups sifted
flour, whole wheat	1 lb.	3½ cups
lemon juice	1 medium	3 tbsp.
lemon rind	1 medium	1 tbsp. grated
nuts, shelled	5 oz.	1 cup
orange juice	1 medium	⅓ cup juice
orange rind	1 medium	2 tbsp.
potatoes, white	1 lb.	3 medium large
raisins	1 lb.	3 cups
rice	1 lb.	2½ cups raw and 3½-4 cups cooked
spaghetti	7 oz.	4 cups cooked, approx.
sugar, brown	1 lb.	2¼ cups
sugar, confectioners'	1 lb.	2¼ cups
sugar, granulated	1 lb.	2 cups
tomatoes	1 lb.	3 medium

Sausalito
Cooking With a View
Part II

Menus with Additional Recipes

The addition of this section to the Revised Second Edition of *Sausalito, Cooking With a View* provides an opportunity to suggest some menus that have been particularly enjoyed at SWC functions and other community events. Please note that the new recipes are not referenced in the main index, they are presented in this Menu section. Other suggested courses are in the book with page numbers in parentheses and are indexed. Enjoy!

Menus

Brunch by the Bay
Frittata Italiano, iii

Ladies' Lunch
Fennel and Mushroom Salad, iv

Linebackers' Feast
Mexican Cole Slaw, v
Corn Bread Mexicana, vi

A Favorite Salmon Supper

An Elegant Valentine's Day Tea
Low-Fat Chocolate Brownies, viii

A Far Eastern Dinner Party
Chicken Tandoori, ix

Savory Summer Supper
Cheese and Tomato Tart, xi

A Mediterranean Dinner
Hummus, xii
Butterflied Leg-of-Lamb, xiii
Zucchini Pie, xiii

Caribbean Company Dinner
Calypso Steak, xv

A California Thanksgiving

Brunch by the Bay

Orange Julia (page 36) and Tomato Juice
Spinach Salad with Basil and Prosciutto (page 64)
Frittata Italiano
Pepper Biscuits (page 185) with Cream Cheese
Sweet-Simit Braided Bread Twists (page 191)
Coffee and Tea

Frittata Italiano

Serves 12.

1½	**cups sliced mushrooms**
4	**tablespoons butter or margarine, divided**
18	**eggs**
9	**tablespoons cream or milk**

Salt and pepper

1	**tablespoon dry basil**
6	**sprigs fresh parsley, minced**
6	**tablespoons Parmesan cheese, divided**
2	**tablespoons olive oil**
1½	**cups diced cooked ham**
12	**ounces mozzarella cheese, cubed**

Preheat oven to 375 degrees. In a large skillet sauté the mushrooms lightly in 2 tablespoons butter. Set aside. In a bowl mix the eggs, cream, salt, pepper, basil, parsley and 3 tablespoons Parmesan cheese. In the same skillet used to cook the mushrooms, heat olive oil and remaining 2 tablespoons of butter. Pour in the egg mixture and cook over low heat while stirring until warmed through and egg mixture just barely starts to cook. (By doing this, when you add the remaining ingredients they won't float to the top of the eggs.) Add the mushrooms, ham and remaining cheeses. Pour into a 9-inch x 13-inch baking dish. Bake until firm about 30 minutes.

Ladies' Lunch

Hedda Hopper's Spill Your Guts Curried Nuts (page 28)
Fennel and Mushroom Salad
Polenta Sandwich (page 128)
Fresh Fruit Tart (page 203)

Fennel and Mushroom Salad

This is a composed salad served at a famous Bay area restaurant.

Serves 6.

1	**pound fresh button mushrooms, sliced**
3	**fresh fennel bulbs (anise)**
½	**cup fresh lemon juice**
½	**cup garlic flavored olive oil**
½	**cup Asiago cheese, shaved**
½	**cup Italian flat leaf parsley, chopped**

Salt and fresh cracked pepper to taste

On individual salad plates, alternate the sliced mushrooms with the thinly sliced fennel. Drizzle the lemon juice and olive oil over each salad. Sprinkle with fresh cracked pepper and salt. Top with the shaved Asiago cheese and parsley. Serve.

Linebacker's Feast

Because everything can be made ahead, the cook can enjoy this hearty menu too. Serve with cold beer and big napkins.

Fiesta Salad (page 57)

Mexican Cole Slaw

Baked Barbecue Spareribs (page 153)

Corn Bread Mexicana

Barbara's Spicy Beer Cake (page 223)

Mexican Cole Slaw

A crispy, crunchy salad that serves an army.

1	head green cabbage
1	head red cabbage
2	carrots, shredded
1	bunch green onions, chopped
2-3	red peppers, chopped
1	cup chopped cilantro
1	can kidney beans, rinsed and drained
2	cups fresh corn, cooked and cut off the cob, or 1 can whole kernel corn, drained
½	bunch radishes, or jicama, sliced
¾	cup rice wine vinegar
4	tablespoons mayonnaise
2	teaspoons celery seed
3	teaspoons sugar

Salt and pepper to taste

Marinated artichoke hearts, optional

In a food processor fitted with a fine blade, slice the cabbages. Change to a chopping blade and pulse the carrots, green onions, peppers and cilantro. Mix together all of the vegetables. Add the remaining ingredients and toss well. Chill at least 2 hours before serving.

Corn Bread Mexicana

Serves 8.

1	cup yellow cornmeal
1	cup all-purpose flour
¼	cup granulated sugar
1	tablespoon baking powder
1	teaspoon salt
1	cup shredded Cheddar cheese
1	cup milk
⅓	cup vegetable oil
1	cup canned corn, drained, or frozen corn
½	cup (4-ounce can) chopped green chiles
1	egg, lightly beaten

Combine cornmeal, flour, sugar, baking powder, salt and Cheddar cheese in a medium bowl; mix well. Combine the milk, oil, corn, green chiles and egg; add to the dry ingredients; stir just until blended. Pour into a well-greased 9-inch square pan. Bake in preheated 400 degree oven for 30 to 35 minutes or until golden brown. Cut into squares and serve warm.

A Favorite Salmon Supper

This is a great entertaining menu with recipes that can be increased to feed a multitude of guests. The salmon may be served hot off the grill or chilled.

Caponata with Baguette Slices (page 86)
Rice Salad with Arugula (page 64)
Grilled Salmon with Red Pepper Sauce (page 174)
Green Vegetables with Hazelnut Dressing (page 87)
Betsy's Lemon Curd Tart (page 204)

An Elegant Valentine's Day Tea

Since its founding almost 100 years ago, the Sausalito Woman's Club has cherished its traditional teas. Each month after the Business Meeting, new members and their sponsors share the duties of preparing and serving a "High Tea," usually for about 50 members. Silver tea and coffee services come out from the kitchen cabinets, flowers arrive from the gardens, and members bring their savories and sweets on attractive plates and platters. A "High Tea" is composed of bite-sized finger food and a tempting feast for the eyes as well as for the mouth. Members gather around the tea table to socialize and plan future projects.

Sandwiches and Savories

Cucumber Sandwiches
Other Tea Sandwiches with Open or Closed Faces
Deviled Eggs
Endive with Smoked Salmon Dip
Mushroom Duxelles and Brie Tartlets (page 25)
Miniature Cream Puffs with Shrimp Salad

Breads

Miniature Lemon Scones (page 199)
Walnut Bread (page 190)
Zucchini Bread
Miniature Orange Almond Muffins (page 195)
Miniature Black Currant Muffins (page 193)
Raspberry Jam, Lemon Curd (page 205), Clotted Cream

Sweets

Heart-shaped Sugar Cookies
Chocolate Cookies
Lace Cookies (page 227)
Almond Macaroons (page 227)
Snickerdoodles (page 235), rolled in red sugar
Madeleines
Pound Cake or Petits Fours
Strawberries
Nuts and Mints
Low-Fat Chocolate Brownies

Low-Fat Chocolate Brownies

Makes 16 to 25 cookies

1⅔ **cups sugar**
½   **cup unsweetened applesauce**
2   **tablespoons water**
4   **ounces unsweetened chocolate, broken up**
2   **eggs, or egg substitute**
1½ **teaspoons vanilla**
1⅓ **cups flour**
¼   **teaspoon baking soda**
¼   **teaspoon salt**
½   **cup nuts, optional**

Heat sugar, applesauce and water in medium saucepan, while stirring constantly, just to a boil. Remove from heat. Add chocolate and stir until melted. Stir in 1 egg at a time until incorporated. Stir in vanilla. Add flour, baking soda and salt, and stir well. Stir in nuts. Pour into 9 x 9-inch baking pan sprayed with cooking spray. Bake in a preheated 350 degree oven for 15 to 20 minutes until wooden toothpick inserted in center comes out slightly sticky. Cool in pan. Cut in desired sizes.

A Far Eastern Dinner Party

Sausalito sits so close to the Pacific Rim that our cuisine is
influenced by many of the exotic tastes and aromas of the Far East.

Minted Citrus Salad (page 56)
Chicken Tandoori
Masala Bhat (page 96)
Hot Curried Fruit (page 212)

Chicken Tandoori

Serves 4 to 6.

SPICE MIX
- ½   teaspoon cumin
- ½   teaspoon ground cardamom
- ½   teaspoon ground coriander
- ½   teaspoon ground cinnamon
- ½   teaspoon ground ginger
- ½   teaspoon fennel seeds
- 1   teaspoon turmeric
- 1   teaspoon white pepper
- 2   tablespoons paprika
- 2   whole dried chili peppers
- 1   green pepper, cored, seeded and cut into pieces
- 1   small onion quartered

CHICKEN AND SAUCE
- 1   cup plain yogurt
- 1   teaspoon salt
- 2   tablespoon lemon juice
- 3   pounds favorite chicken pieces

Put all of the spice mix ingredients in a food processor, blending well. In a large bowl, mix the yogurt, salt and lemon juice. Add the spice mix and stir well. Add the chicken and marinate 8 hours or overnight. Grill or broil 10 to 15 minutes on each side, or until done.

Savory Summer Supper

*You can prepare this menu a day ahead. It's great after a
day on the Bay or hiking in the Marin Headlands.*

Green Salad

Crunchy Pea Salad (page 61)

Cheese and Tomato Tart

World's Easiest Apple Cake (page 222)

Cheese and Tomato Tart

Serves 6 to 8.

PASTRY
5   ounces flour (about 1 cup)
Pinch salt
Pinch sugar
6   tablespoons cold butter
2   tablespoons solid shortening
3   tablespoons cold water
Dijon mustard

FILLING
3   medium tomatoes, cut into ¼-inch slices
Salt
¾   pound Gruyère or Swiss cheese, coarsely grated
Freshly ground pepper
2   tablespoons chopped fresh basil
2   tablespoons freshly grated Parmesan cheese
2   tablespoons butter, melted

Put flour, salt, sugar, butter and shortening in mixing bowl. Mix together with a pastry blender until coarse and crumbly. Then add water and quickly form into a smooth mass. Roll out and line a 9-inch quiche pan or tart pan and refrigerate for at least 1 hour. Cover pastry with foil. Add pastry weights and bake in a preheated 425 degree oven for 15 minutes until the pastry has set. Remove weights and foil and bake for 10 additional minutes. Remove from oven. Reduce oven temperature to 375 degrees.

Place sliced tomatoes on rack. Sprinkle with salt and let drain for 30 minutes. Brush pastry shell with Dijon mustard. Arrange grated cheese on top. Lay tomato slices side by side without overlapping. Sprinkle with pepper, basil and Parmesan cheese. Drizzle melted butter over top. Bake in 375 degree oven for 30 minutes until cheese has melted. Let stand 5 minutes before slicing. This tart can be reheated nicely.

A Mediterranean Dinner

*A delicious menu any time of the year, wonderful for a special
occasion or holiday meal. These recipes serve 8 comfortably.*

Hummus
Agnes' Stuffed Grape Leaves (page 26)
Barbecued Butterflied Leg-of-Lamb
Armenian Rice Pilaf (page 95, double recipe for 8)
Zucchini Pie
Lemon Chiffon Cheesecake (page 210)

Hummus

1	can garbanzo beans, drained
¼	cup Tahini (sesame paste, available in most supermarkets, or ¼ cup sesame seeds)
2	cloves garlic, peeled
¼	cup fresh lemon juice
¼	cup olive oil

Salt and pepper to taste
Dash of cumin
Paprika for garnish
Pita pocket bread cut into triangles (may be toasted)

Put all of the ingredients except the paprika and Pita bread into a
food processor and process until smooth. Spread on a flat plate or
serve in a bowl. Sprinkle with paprika. Surround with Pita bread
triangles and serve. This can be made several days in advance and
refrigerated until ready to serve.

Barbecued Butterflied Leg-of-Lamb

This marinade uses just a few ingredients but delivers a lot of flavor.
It works equally well on chicken.

1	**leg of lamb, boned, butterflied and trimmed of excess fat**
¼	**cup olive oil**
¼	**cup soy sauce**
¼	**cup lemon juice**
3	**cloves of garlic, peeled and crushed**
1	**tablespoon of oregano**

Salt and pepper to taste

Mix the marinade ingredients together and pour over the lamb. Marinate 8 hours or overnight. Preheat the barbecue. The coals should be hot. Place meat on grill and cook for 20 minutes each side for medium to medium rare, or 25 to 30 minutes each side for medium to well-done. Allow meat to rest 10 to15 minutes. Slice and serve. This may also be served at room temperature.

Zucchini Pie

6	**small zucchini, thinly sliced**
1	**cup Bisquick mix**
½	**cup olive oil**
4	**eggs, slightly beaten**
½	**cup grated Parmesan or Asiago cheese**
½	**cup finely chopped onion**
2	**tablespoons parsley, minced**
1	**garlic clove, finely minced**
½	**teaspoon oregano**
½	**teaspoon mixed herbs seasoning**
½	**teaspoon salt**

Preheat the oven to 350 degrees. Mix all of the ingredients together and spread in a greased 13 x 9 x 2-inch heat resistant glass casserole. Bake 30 minutes until slightly browned. Delicious with any meat or chicken entrée and equally tasty as a vegetarian dish served with a salad and bread.

Caribbean Company Dinner

Champagne and Rum Tropical Punch (page 35), Wine, Beer
Sweet Potato Chips (page 22) and Seasoned Nuts
Prawns with Lime Mayonnaise (page 30)
Green Salad
Barbecued Pork with Tropical Fruit Salsa (page 151)
Calypso Steak
Green Rice
Black Beans
A selection of tropical fruits and sorbets

Calypso Steak

Serves 8.

1½-2 **pounds boneless beef top sirloin or top round steak, cut 1-inch thick**

MARINADE

½ **medium onion, cut into quarters**

¼ **cup honey**

¼ **cup fresh lime juice**

10-12 quarter-size slices fresh ginger

1-2 jalapeño peppers, cut in half

3 cloves garlic

½ **teaspoon ground allspice**

½ **teaspoon paprika**

½ **teaspoon dried thyme**

Place marinade ingredients in blender or food processor and whirl until blended. Place beef in marinade in plastic bag, turning to coat. Close bag securely and marinate in refrigerator 30 minutes to 2 hours, turning once. Remove steak from marinade; reserve marinade. Barbecue to desired doneness.

In small saucepan bring marinade to a rolling boil over high heat. Boil two minutes; strain and use for sauce. Carve steak into thin slices. Arrange on serving platters. Garnish with edible flowers for a tropical touch, if desired. Serve with sauce.

A California Thanksgiving

Some of these recipes were featured in a Thanksgiving cooking demonstration by Jerry Anne Di Vecchio, Senior Food Editor of Sunset Magazine, *that celebrated the launching of our cookbook.*

Southeast Asian Peanut Dip (page 15) and Crudités

Wine-Basted Barbecued Turkey (page 167),
baked in oven, if desired

Red Pepper Relish (page 248) and Cranberry Sauce

Festive Onions (page 89)

Sweet Potato and Orange Casserole (page 91)
or Plain Yams

Macadamia Nut Pie (page 208)

Index

C

N

Sausalito Woman's Club Cookbook

P.O. Box 733
Sausalito, CA 94966

Please send _____ copy(ies) of
 Sausalito Cooking with a View   @ $25.00 each _____

 Postage and handling for first book   @ $ 4.00 each _____

 Each additional book
  shipped to same address   @ $ 1.50 each _____

 California residents add sales tax   @ $ 1.80 each _____

 TOTAL _____

Name _____

Address _____

City _____ State _____ Zip _____

Please make checks payable to SWC Cookbook
Thank you for your order!

- -

Sausalito Woman's Club Cookbook

P.O. Box 733
Sausalito, CA 94966

Please send _____ copy(ies) of
 Sausalito Cooking with a View   @ $25.00 each _____

 Postage and handling for first book   @ $ 4.00 each _____

 Each additional book
  shipped to same address   @ $ 1.50 each _____

 California residents add sales tax   @ $ 1.80 each _____

 TOTAL _____

Name _____

Address _____

City _____ State _____ Zip _____

Please make checks payable to SWC Cookbook
Thank you for your order!